Student Workbook

for

Verderber and Verderber's

Communicate!

Eleventh Edition

Student Workbook

for

Verderber and Verderber's

Communicate!

Eleventh Edition

Leonard E. Assante
Volunteer State Community College

THOMSON

WADSWORTH

Australia • Canada • Mexico • Singapore • Spain • United Kingdom • United States

Printed in the United States of America
1 2 3 4 5 6 7 07 06 05 04

Printer: Thomson West

0-534-63939-9

For more information about our products,
contact us at:
Thomson Learning Academic Resource Center
1-800-423-0563

For permission to use material from this text or product, submit a request online at
http://www.thomsonrights.com
Any additional questions about permissions can be submitted at
thomsonrights@thomson.com

Thomson Wadsworth
10 Davis Drive
Belmont, CA 94002-3098
USA

Asia
Thomson Learning
5 Shenton Way #01-01
UIC Building
Singapore 068808

Australia/New Zealand
Thomson Learning
102 Dodds Street
Southbank, Victoria 3006
Australia

Canada
Nelson
1120 Birchmount Road
Toronto, Ontario M1K 5G4
Canada

Europe/Middle East/South Africa
Thomson Learning
High Holborn House
50/51 Bedford Row
London WC1R 4LR
United Kingdom

Latin America
Thomson Learning
Seneca, 53
Colonia Polanco
11560 Mexico D.F.
Mexico

Spain/Portugal
Paraninfo
Calle/Magallanes, 25
28015 Madrid, Spain

TABLE OF CONTENTS

Acknowledgments

Preface

PART I: FOUNDATIONS OF COMMUNICATION

PART II: INTERPERSONAL COMMUNICATION

PART III: GROUP COMMUNICATION

CHAPTER 10: Participating in Group Communication
Learning Objectives
Interactive Chapter Outline
Key Terms
Activities
Chapter Self Test
Helpful Links

CHAPTER 11: Member Roles and Leadership in Groups
Learning Objectives
Interactive Chapter Outline
Key Terms
Activities
Chapter Self Test
Helpful Links

PART IV: PUBLIC SPEAKING

CHAPTER 12: Determining Your Speaking Goal
Learning Objectives
Interactive Chapter Outline
Key Terms
Activities
Chapter Self Test
Helpful Links

CHAPTER 13: Doing Research
Learning Objectives
Interactive Chapter Outline
Key Terms
Activities
Chapter Self Test
Helpful Links

CHAPTER 14: Organizing
Learning Objectives
Interactive Chapter Outline
Key Terms
Activities

Chapter Self Test
Helpful Links

Learning Objectives
Interactive Chapter Outline
Key Terms
Activities
Chapter Self Test
Helpful Links

Learning Objectives
Interactive Chapter Outline
Key Terms
Activities
Diagnostic Speech Checklist
Chapter Self Test
Helpful Links

Learning Objectives
Interactive Chapter Outline
Key Terms
Activities
Chapter Self Test
Helpful Links

Learning Objectives
Interactive Chapter Outline
Key Terms
Activities
Chapter Self Test
Helpful Links

ACKNOWLEDGEMENTS

Many people have assisted me in preparing my second student workbook for the *Communicate!* text. As with the first, without their help, this text would not be as thorough and useful as it is! I would like to specifically acknowledge the following:

-*Deirdre Anderson*
-*Breanna Gilbert-Gambacorta*
 -*Stuart Schrader*
-*Cindy McLeod*
-*The faculty of the Department of Communication* at Volunteer State Community College

-And especially to all of those colleagues across the country who have offered feedback —all constructive- since the release of the first workbook. I hope this new edition is useful.

-*Leonard Assante*, January 1, 2004, Gallatin, TN

PREFACE

Welcome to the Student Workbook for *Communicate! Eleventh Edition* by Rudolph and Kathleen Verderber! Congratulations on your decision to enroll in an introductory communication course. Effective communication skills are an important component to a successful career and satisfying interpersonal relationships. When I decided to accept the offer to write this companion volume, I knew that for it to be a truly useful addition to the text (they call it an "ancillary" in the book business), students had to actually *use* it. And use it *regularly*. And use it *often*. The publisher also sent me copies of other "student workbooks" that had been written for other texts. In each of these, I found useful and interesting ideas. What I decided I would try to do was create a book that was hopefully more than a workbook, but actually a companion guide to the textbook that incorporates both my own ideas and the best of what I have found in reviewing other similar texts. My hope is that you will find this approach useful in your study of communication. This Student Workbook" is designed to be used with the textbook in studying for exams, learning key concepts, doing application exercises, researching speeches and taking notes in class. I encourage you to take this book to class along with your textbook, use it to help you take notes, to tie the individual concepts together into the "big picture," and to assist your communication education. Below I list the key objectives of the textbook and course. I then introduce you to the key parts of this book and how they are designed to help you. Good luck!

Textbook Objectives. The textbook is designed to meet several objectives;
- To make the communication process understood by defining and clarifying key terms used to talk about communication.
- To apply communication concepts to situations we encounter in our everyday lives.
- To present guidelines for communication competency and skill development.

Course Objectives. While all communication courses (and communication instructors!) are different, it is very likely that any course that uses *Communicate!* has the following objectives:
- Define and describe the communication process.
- Relate self-perception and behaviors to verbal and non-verbal communication.
- Recognize various meanings of verbal, vocal, and non-verbal symbols and their effect on interpersonal relationships.
- Describe conversations related skills, including in electronically mediated contexts.
- Identify methods of dealing with conflict in interpersonal relationships.
- List and describe effective techniques for communicating ideas and feelings.
- List and define guidelines for effective listening and responding techniques.

- Describe the nature and stages of relationships.
- Describe the interviewing process and related interpersonal skills
- Identify the process and procedures of decision-making in groups.
- Identify leadership styles
- Identify steps for personal leadership development
- Identify key techniques for successful interviews
- Prepare and deliver an informative speech
- Prepare and deliver a persuasive speech

This student companion contains the following components:

Learning Objectives. Each chapter begins with a short list of objectives for that chapter. These are written in the form "After studying this chapter you should be able to…". The idea here is to give you an idea of what your instructor expects you to understand when the chapter is completed. Think of it as a list of your goals for that chapter. The sample test questions are based on these.

Interactive Chapter Outline. This is a detailed outline of the corresponding textbook chapter. It includes space for you to write your own notes. Use it as a guide to the organization of each chapter and to help you takes notes in class or while reading. Research suggests that students learn better if they can concentrate more on the concepts themselves and less on how they are organized when taking notes. The interactive outline provides the organizational structure, allowing you to concentrate on the individual terms and ideas.

Key Terms. A list of all terms highlighted and defined in the margins of the textbook is presented here. Space is provided for you to write in the definition, examples, or additional notes. Looking up and writing out the definitions of these terms is an excellent study aid and helps to build your vocabulary. Test questions often use these terms.

Activities. One of the most important features of this companion is the selection of chapter exercises. These activities are designed to help you understand and apply the key ideas and concepts from each chapter. There are several different types of exercises. These include:

InfoTrac and Internet-based: These activities make use of technology, the Internet and *InfoTrac College Edition*, an Internet-based research resource you will find useful when seeking additional information on key concepts or when doing research for speeches or projects. This text contains all exercises found in the textbook as well as additional activities.

Observe and analyze: In selected locations throughout the textbook are the *Observe and Analyze* icons. These prompt you to complete a journal activity in this workbook. All the necessary journal forms are located in this text.

Chapter Self Test. True/false, multiple choice, and short essay questions are provided. These questions are designed to be similar to those you might encounter in an examination. Page references are provided in the answer key so you may check your work. If you think any of my answers are incorrect or my questions misleading, let me know. My students do!

Helpful Links. At the end of each chapter I list several useful or interesting Internet links that are relevant to the material covered in that chapter. I have collected these over the years and have "borrowed" many from colleagues. Feel free to check them out. All links were accurate and current at the time of writing. If you find a "dead link", let me know.

Miscellaneous Resources. Some chapters include other materials in addition to those listed above. This is especially true in the Group Communication and Public Speaking chapters.

I hope this text is useful to you. Please let me know what you think so I can make future editions even more useful.

Leonard Assante
Department of Communication
Volunteer State Community College
Gallatin, TN 37066
Len.Assante@volstate.edu

I

FOUNDATIONS OF COMMUNICATION

CHAPTER 1: Communication Perspectives

Learning Objectives

After studying this chapter, you should be able to answer these questions:

- What is the definition of communication?
- How does the communication process work?
- Why do we communicate?
- What characterizes each of the communication settings you will study in this course?
- What are six basic principles of communication?
- Why should a communicator be concerned about diversity?
- What major ethical issues face communicators?
- What is communication competence?
- How can you improve your communication skills?

Interactive Chapter Outline

I. The Communication Process

    A. Definition of Communication

    _____

    _____

    B. Participants

    _____

    _____

    C. Contexts

    _____

    _____

        1. Physical Context

_____

2. Social Context

_____

3. Historical Context

_____

4. Psychological Context

_____

5. Cultural Context

_____

D. Messages

_____

_____

1. Meaning

_____

2. Symbols

_____

3. Encoding

_____

4. Decoding

_____

5. Form or organization

_____

E. Channels

_____

_____

F. Noise

_____

_____

    1. External Noises

_____

    2. Internal Noises

_____

    3. Semantic Noises

_____

G. Feedback

_____

_____

II. Communication Functions and Settings
    A. Communication Functions

_____

_____

    1. _____

    2. _____

    3. _____

    4. _____

    5. _____

B. Communication Settings

_____

_____

    1. _____

    2. _____

    3. _____

    4. _____

III. Communication Principles
    A. Communication has Purpose

_____

_____

B. Communication is Continuous

_____

_____

C. Communication Messages vary in Conscious Thought

_____

_____

D. Communication is Relational

_____

_____

    1.

    _____

    2. _____

E. Communication is Guided by Culture

_____

_____

F. Communication has Ethical Implications

_____

_____

    1. Ethics

    _____

    2. Truthfulness and Honesty

    _____

    3. Integrity

_____

4. Fairness

_____

5. Respect

_____

6. Responsibility

_____

G. Communication is Learned

_____

_____

IV. Increasing our Communication Competence
   A. Writing Goal Statements

_____

_____

     1.

_____

     2.

_____

     3.

_____

     4.

_____

Key Terms

8

communication (p. 4)

_____

_____

participants (p. 4)

_____

_____

context (p. 5)

_____

_____

physical context (p. 5)

_____

_____

social context (p. 5)

_____

_____

historical context (p. 5)

_____

_____

psychological context (p. 6)

_____

_____

cultural context (p. 6)

_____

_____

message (p. 6)

meaning (p. 6)

symbols (p. 6)

encoding (p. 7)

decoding (p. 7)

channel (p. 7)

noise (p. 7)

external noises (p. 7)

internal noises (p. 7)

_____

_____

semantic noises (p. 7)

_____

_____

feedback (p. 7)

_____

_____

interpersonal communication settings (p. 10)

_____

_____

problem-solving group settings (p. 11)

_____

_____

public-speaking settings (p. 11)

_____

_____

electronically mediated communication settings (p. 11)

_____

_____

email (p. 11)

_____

_____

newsgroup (p. 11)

Internet chat (p. 12)

spontaneous (p.13)

scripted message (p. 13)

constructed message (p. 13)

immediacy (p. 13)

control (p. 14)

cultural diversity (p. 14)

ethics (p. 16)

truthfulness & honesty (p. 17)

moral dilemma (p. 17)

integrity (p. 17)

fairness (p. 17)

respect (p. 17)

responsibility (p. 17)

communication competence (p. 18)

skills (p. 20)

Exercises

Activity 1.1 - Test Your Competence: Identifying Elements of the Communication Process (p. 9)

For the interaction described on page 9, identify the context, participants, channel, message, noise and feedback.

1.Contexts:

   Physical:

   Social:

   Historical:

   Psychological:

   Cultural:

2. Participants:

3. Channels:

4. Message:

5. Noise:

6. Feedback:

Activity 1.2 - Observe and Analyze: Communication Functions

Using the worksheet that follows, keep a log of the various communications you have today. Tonight, categorize each episode by one of the six functions it served. Each episode may serve more than one function. Were you surprised by the variety of communication you engaged in such a relatively short period? (You can download additional blank log sheets from the *Communicate!* web site.)

Communication Functions Log

Conversational partner(s)	Social needs	Sense of self	Develop relationship	Exchange information	Influence others
Cindy	X			X	

Activity 1.3 - Conversations

Think of two recent conversations you participated in, one that you thought went really well and one that you thought went poorly. Compare them using the form that follows. Describe the context in which the conversations occurred, the participants, the rules that seemed to govern your behavior and that of the other participants, the messages that were used to create the meaning and, the channels used, any noise that interfered with communication, the feedback that was shared, and the result.

Activity 1.3 Worksheet.   Name:_____

	Conversation that Went Well	Conversation that Went Poorly
Context		
Participants		
Rules		
Messages		
Channel		
Noise		
Feedback		
End Result		

Activity 1.4 – Use of Email

Do you use Email? Consider the mailing you have done over the last week. Using the worksheet that follows, classify the kinds of messages you have written (use such headings as letters to friends, inquiries to Web sites, questions to professors, and so forth). How many messages do you receive each day? What percentage of those do you reply to? Compare your email use to regular mail. How many letters (not bills, advertisements or solicitations) do you send or receive each day?

Activity 1.4 Worksheet.   Name:_____

Email:

Kinds of messages written over the past week:

1.

2.

3.

4.

5.

How many messages do you receive each day? _____

Percentage that you reply to: _____

Email vs. regular mail:

How many letters do you send or receive each day?   Send: ___ Receive: ___

1.5 Using InfoTrac College Edition

Cultural issues play an important role in global business. For example, in the airline industry gate agents, flight attendants and other service providers must be able to communicate effectively with people who come from different cultures and speak different languages. Using InfoTrac College Edition, you can find an interesting article on this subject. After typing in "Intercultural Communication" as the Subject Guide, locate the article "Plane Talk," by John Freivalds. Read what the airline industry is doing to make language learning a priority among flight attendants and pilots. How is this training working to achieve industry goals?

1.6 Using InfoTrac College Edition.

The ability to communicate in complex ways is often seen as a key difference between humans and lower animals. Using InfoTrac College Edition, type in "human communication" as the subject guide and locate articles that contrast human and animal communication. Then list what you perceive to be three key differences between animal and human communication. (Remember to use the "View other articles linked to these subjects" function to assist your search.)

1.7 Using the Web (p. 21).
To learn more about ethics, use your Communicate! CD-ROM to access Web Resource 1.3: Ethics Connection at the Communicate! Website. Select the chapter resources for Chapter 1, then click on "Web Resources." This site is sponsored by the Markkula Center for Applied Ethics at Santa Clara University.
http://www.scu.edu/scu/centers/ethics/

1.8 Using the Web.   Using the links listed at the end of this chapter, browse through some of the sites devoted to the study and research of communication. Are you surprised by how many sites there are? About the amount of research being done in the field? About the different types of communication specialties? Pick any two sites and write a brief comparison essay. Focus on the content and organization of the two sites. What did you learn from your visits?

1.9 Analyzing Feedback. Keep a one-day log of all the feedback (verbal and nonverbal) you receive from others while communicating. Ask someone who knows you well to indicate the kinds of feedback you typically give him or her while they communicate with you. Analyze the similarities and differences in the feedback you give and receive.

1.10 Diagram a Communication Event. Using the model of communication presented on page 8 in your text, diagram a recent conversation you had. Who were the participants? What messages were sent? Using what channels? What feedback was given? Was there any noise present? In what context did the communication take place. Draw a diagram of the model and insert each answer in the correct location.

1.11 Communication Settings. After reviewing the four communication settings discussed on pages 10-12, identify the setting you feel you are most effective in and why you feel that way. Which setting are you least effective in? Why? Using the example found on page 22 as a guide, develop a Communication Improvement Plan to help you increase your competence in the communication setting you feel least effective in.

1.12 What Would You Do? A Question of Ethics (pp 22-23). Read the scenario in the text and answer the question at the end of the story. Check your answer by reviewing pages 16-18.

Chapter 1 Self Test (answers and page references in Appendix)

True/False

1. The mood and feelings each person brings to the conversation is called "psychological context."

2. The process of transforming messages from another back into one's own ideas is called "encoding."

3. The route traveled by a message is called context.

4. The major criteria for determining communication competence are successful and concrete.

5. A salesperson giving reasons why you should purchase a product is an example of how communication has purpose.

6. Communication is continuous.

7. Skills are goal-oriented actions or action sequences that we can master and repeat.

8. Fairness means showing regard or consideration for others.

Multiple Choice

1. The fact that you are likely to take legal advice from your lawyer is a good example of the importance of _____ to communication.
   a. physical context
   b. social context
   c. complementary context
   d. fairness

2. The process of creating or sharing meaning is called
   a. communicating
   b. encoding
   c. transmitting
   d. decoding
   e. receiving

3. At dinner, you ask your brother's advice on whether you should take philosophy or anthropology to meet a course requirement at school. The next day, when you see your brother again, you say "I decided on philosophy." Your roommate's understanding of that message is explained by
   a. physical context
   b. historical context

c. psychological context
d. noise

4. If a person is thinking about the great time she had last night while listening to a class lecture, these thoughts would be considered
   a. encoding
   b. decoding
   c. feedback
   d. noise
   e. none of the above

5. Which of the following is considered an ethical question?
   a. Saul gives Maria a reward for finding his lost dog.
   b. Juan takes Leonard's book out of his bag.
   c. Cindy tells her friends she bought the food for lunch when in fact Amanda did.
   d. Joe punches Nick in the arm.

6. Juanita walks into a room and sees her two children arguing over a toy. She listens patiently and openly while allowing both children to explain their side of the story. Juanita is exemplifying which ethical implication of communication?
   a. respect
   b. fairness
   c. responsibility
   d. integrity
   e. moral imperative

7. According to Samovar and Porter, which three cultural elements have the potential to affect situations in which people from different backgrounds come together?
   a. perception, communication, context
   b. communication, context, respect
   c. nonverbal processes, context, communication
   d. verbal processes, psychological context, cultural context
   e. perception, verbal processes, nonverbal processes

8. Mandy is preparing a speech on a complex chemical process for her Organic Chemistry class. She spends a great deal of time deciding the order of main ideas, the use of examples, and preparing summary statements. Mandy's project is a good example of the importance of what aspect of messages?
   a. form or organization
   b. channel
   c. noise
   d. decoding

Essay

1. Explain how the different types of noise affect meaning.

2. Describe the six different parts of the communication process.

3. What are the functions of communication? Provide at least one example of each function.

4. Describe a "moral dilemma." Provide an example. Why do many people lie when in a moral dilemma?

Helpful Links

http://www.natcom.org - **National Communication Association (NCA)**
NCA is the largest organization of communication students, researchers and teachers. This site previews some of the activities communication scholars engage in and offers a variety of links to other sources.

http://www.cios.org - **Communication Institute for Online Scholarship (CIOS)**
CIOS provides discussion in a variety of current issues in the filed of communication, links to extensive resources and links designed especially for students.

http://www.mapnp.org/library/grp_skll/grp_skll.htm - **Group Skills**
A selection of web resources assembled by Carter McNamara of the Management Assistance Program for Non-Profits, this site lists numerous resources for group dynamics and problem-solving.

http://www.hack.gr/jargon/ - **Jargon –The New Hacker's Dictionary**
This link is one of many on the net to one version or another of "The New Hacker's Dictionary," a list of the slang of the computer user and the computer-mediated-communication user.

http://www.toastmasters.org/pdfs/top10.pdf - **Ten Tips for Effective Public Speaking**
This guide created by Toastmaster's International shows the importance of understanding the setting when making oral presentations. Part of the Toastmaster's website http://www.toastmasters.org

(See your Communicate! CD-ROM for links to other websites referenced in your text.)

CHAPTER 2: Perception of Self and Others

After studying this chapter, you should be able to answer these questions:
- What perception?
- How does your mind select, organize and interpret information?
- What is the self-concept and how is it formed?
- What is self-esteem and how is it developed?
- How do self-concept and self-esteem affect our communication with others?
- Why affects how accurately you perceive others?
- What are some methods for improving the accuracy of your social perception?

Interactive Chapter Outline

I. The Perception Process

    A. Attention and Selection

_____

_____

        1. Needs

_____

        2. Interest

_____

        3. Expectation

_____

    B. Organization of Stimuli

_____

_____

      1. Simplicity

_____

      2. Pattern

_____

  C. Interpretation of Stimuli

_____

_____

II. Perception of Self: Self-Concept and Self-Esteem
    A. Forming and Maintaining a Self-Concept

_____

_____

      1. Self-Perception

_____

      2. Reactions and responses of others

_____

  B. Developing and Maintaining Self-Esteem

_____

_____

  C. Accuracy of Self-Concept and Self-Esteem

_____

_____

      1. Incongruence

_____

2. Self-fulfilling prophecies

_____

3. Filtering Messages

_____

4. Changing self-concept and self-esteem

_____

D. Self-Concept and Self-Esteem and Communication

_____

_____

   1. _____

   2. _____

E. Presenting Ourselves

_____

_____

F. Cultural and Gender Differences

_____

_____

III. Perception of Others
   A. Observing Physical Characteristics and Social Behaviors

_____

_____

   1. Implicit personality theories

_____

2. Halo effect

_____

B. Using Stereotypes

_____

_____

1. Prejudice

_____

2. Discrimination

_____

3. Racism, ethnocentrism, sexism, ageism, able-ism

_____

C. Emotional States

_____

_____

1. Attributions

_____

D. Improving Social Perception

_____

_____

1. Question the accuracy of your perceptions

_____

2. Seek more information to verify perceptions

3. Realize that your perceptions of a person will change over time

E. Perception Checking

Key Terms

perception (p. 28)

pattern (p. 29)

interpret (p. 29)

self-concept (p. 30)

self-esteem (p. 30)

incongruence (p. 33)

self-fulfilling prophecies (p. 33)

self-talk (p. 34)

role (p. 35)

uncertainty reduction (p. 37)

implicit personality theories (p. 38)

halo effect (p. 38)

stereotypes (p. 38)

prejudice (p. 39)

discrimination (p. 39)

_____

_____

racism, ethnocentrism, sexism, ageism, able-ism, & other "-isms" (p. 40)

_____

_____

attributions (p. 43)

_____

_____

perception check (p. 44)

_____

_____

Exercises

Activity 2.1 Observe and Analyze: Who am I? (p. 32-33)

Using the directions found on page 32-33 of your textbook, complete the following two worksheets. The worksheets may also be found online by using your Communicate! CD-ROM.

Self Perception Worksheet

I am skilled at	I have the ability to	I know things about	I am competent at doing	By personality I am

Others' Perceptions Worksheet

Others believe that I am skilled at	Others believe I have the ability to	Others believe I know things about	Others believe I am competent at doing	Others believe that my personality is

Activity 2.2 Observe and Analyze: Monitor Your Enacted Roles (p. 36-37)
Using the directions found on page 32-33 of your textbook, complete the following worksheet. The worksheet may also be found online by using your Communicate! CD-ROM.

Enacted Roles Data Collection Sheet

Day	Time frame	Situation	Enacted role

Activity 2.3 – Who Am I?
Compare your self-perception and others' perception lists from Activity 2.1. How are these lists similar? Where are they different? Do you understand why they are different? Are your lists long or short? Why do you suppose that is? Reflect on how your own interpretations of your experiences and what others have told you about you have influenced your self-concept. Now organize the lists you created, perhaps finding a way to group characteristics. Use this information to write an essay titled "Who I am, and how I know this." If you wish, use the table below to help organize your thoughts.

CATEGORY	SELF-PERCEPTION	OTHER-PERCEPTION
Skills		
Abilities		
Knowledge		
Competencies		
Personality Characteristics		

2.4 Using the Web (p. 34)

Many books have been written to help people raise their self esteem and there are rich sources of information available on the World Wide Web. To check out one such source, Coping.org's Model of Self Esteem program, use your Communicate! CD-ROM to access Web Resource 2.1: Self Esteem Model at the Communicate Website.

2.5 Using the Web

The internet has numerous sites and pages devoted to material on self-concept and self-esteem. Some sites review research, others offer practical advice and opinions. One particularly provocative opinion is that of Dr. Richard O'Connor in his statement entitled "Self-Esteem: in a culture where winning is everything and losing is shameful." The key question he asks is whether self-esteem as a general construct is always helpful. What points does Dr. O'Connor make? How does his conclusion square with what you have observed? To open his statement, go to
http://www.pioneerthinking.com/esteem.html

2.6 Using InfoTrac College Edition

Some people believe that the media influence our perception of self and others. What does research show? Using InfoTrac College Edition, look under the subject "Self-evaluation." See Female "thin ideal" media images and boys' attitudes toward girls. *Duane A. Hargreaves; Marika Tiggemann. Sex Roles: A Journal of Research*, Nov 2003 v49 i9-10 p539(6). Can you find additional related studies? Summarize what you find in the space below.

2.7 Using InfoTrac College Edition

Using InfoTrac College Edition, look up the subject of Self-Esteem. Find the article "Extending Social Comparison: An Examination of the Unintended Consequences of Idealized Advertising Imagery" *Journal of Advertising*, Summer 2000 v29 i2 p17. In the space below, summarize the findings. Were you surprised about the impact of idealized images of physical attractiveness on males? Why or why not?

2.8 Using the Web.

About.com's psychology section has a large selection of articles related to perception. Go to http://psychology.about.com/science/psychology/cs/percep/index.htm and click on "Perception online tutorials," then "Vision and Art" to learn about how artists use elements of perception when creating art. Write a brief essay summarizing what you have learned from the tutorial and relating it to the material discussed in Chapter 2 of your textbook. Are you surprised that artists study perception and use what they have learned when creating two-dimensional designs?

2.9 Accuracy and Inaccuracy in Perception.

Some perceptions are not always accurate. To test this idea, do the following activity. Record your work on the worksheet that follows.

A. Observe several other students in your classes in an attempt to determine their mood. Choose both students you know well as well as those you don't know.

B. Using the three-step process of perception as outlines in Chapter 2, do the following:
1. *Attend* and *select* stimuli. List what items you focused on.7
2. *Organize* the stimuli. Look for any patterns in behavior. What did you observe?
3. *Interpret* the stimuli. What conclusion have you come to concerning his/her mood?

C. Finally, check your perception. Ask the students you observed to confirm your perception. Note the stimuli you observed and the conclusion you came to. Is each student's mood what you thought it would be?

2.9 Accuracy and Inaccuracy in Perception Worksheet. Name: _____

Stimuli	Patterns	Interpretation	Know/ Not Know?	Accurate?

2.10 Culture and Self-Esteem/Self-Concept.

Imagine you live in a culture which values age over youth and group over individual. In a brief essay, speculate as to how your life would be different than it is now. Are these differences positive, negative, both or neither? If you live in such a culture, reverse the assignment.

2.11 Knowledge of Self.

Read each of the following scenarios. Put yourself in each situation and answer the questions for each.

Situation: A friend and classmate asks if you want a copy of a stolen answer sheet he has for an upcoming exam in your next class. *How do you answer?*

Situation: Someone you are really attracted to has just asked you out to a dance, but you had already agreed to do something with a friend that evening. *How do you answer?*

Questions:

1. What role did your self-concept play in your responses?

2. What role did others' possible impressions of your behavior play in your responses?

2.12 What Would You Do? A question of Ethics (p. 46)

Read the scenario on page 46 in your textbook. Answer the questions at the end in the space below. Your essay should include a plan for Mr. Hernandez and discuss how he can use social perceptions.

Chapter 2 Self Test (answers and page references in Appendix)

True/False

1. Selectively attending to information and assigning meaning to it is called perception.

2. As you get ready for the big game, you say to yourself, "I know I wont play well today, I'm too stressed," and you end up playing poorly. This is an example of a self-fulfilling prophecy.

3. The three steps of the perception process are selection, retention and attention.

4. Self-concept and self-esteem are essentially the same.

5. It is possible to improve our perceptions.

6. Prejudice and discrimination are synonymous.

7. Our emotional state at the time of a perception may influence that perception.

Multiple Choice

1. Self-esteem is defined in your text as
    a. our overall evaluation of our competence and personal worthiness
    b. the list of characteristics that define who we are
    c. part of the self-perception process that never changes
    d. all of the above

2. Jamie decides the flashing red light in his rear-view mirror means she must pull over to the side of the road. This is an example of
    a. selection
    b. attending
    c. interpretation
    d. roles
    e. stereotyping

3. The richer our self-concept
    a. the higher our self-esteem
    b. the lower our self-esteem
    c. the better we are at the selection phase of perception
    d. the better we know and understand who we are

4. Suppose you prepare a meal for several friends. One of them comments that you are a good cook. You ignore the message or reply, "It was nothing special, anyone could have made that meal." This is an example of
    a. self-fulfilling prophecy
    b. how we may distort self-perceptions by filtering messages
    c. a negative role
    d. halo effect

5. You just received your income tax refund. You are in a very good mood all day. As a result you tend to see other people and events in a more positive way than you might otherwise. This is an example of
    a. how emotional states influence our perception
    b. halo effect
    c. roles
    d. none of the above

6. Which of the following is not a way of improving social perceptions?
    a. questioning the accuracy of your perceptions
    b. ignoring information that does not fit a pattern
    c. seeking more information to verify perceptions
    d. realize that your perceptions of a person will change over time

7. A role is:
    a. a pattern of learned behaviors that people use to meet the perceived demands of a given context
    b. enacted based on our own needs and relationships
    c. something we only enact one of each day
    d. a and b

8. You make a dinner date with your best friend for 7pm. It is now 7:30pm and they have not shown up yet. You guess that your friend had something come up that they have no control over. This is an example of:
    a. improved social perception
    b. social role
    c. attribution
    d. self-presentation

Essay

1. Contrast self-perception and self-esteem

2. Describe how we can improve our perception ability. Offer at least one example.

3. Contrast the "Western view of self" with the "Eastern View of Self." Provide an example to illustrate your contrast.

4. Define stereotypes and discuss the role they play in our perception of others.

5. What are the different ways we have of improving our social perceptions? Provide an example of each.

Helpful Links

http://www.adiosbarbie.com – **Adios Barbie**
This site looks at self-esteem by discussing the "Barbie image" and its effect on women and men.

http://www.parascope.com/articles/0397/sublim.htm - **The Subliminal Scares**
This link connects to an article on the impact of subliminal meanings on the perception process.

http://www.mentalhelp.net/psyhelp/chap7/chap7l.htm - **Disliking Others Without Valid Reasons: Prejudice**
Material from the book *Psychological Self Help* by Clayton Tucker-Ladd helps the reader understand the roots of prejudice.

http://www.mentalhelp.net/psyhelp/chap14/chap14d.htm - **Changing your Self-Concept and building Self Esteem**
Another set of material from Tucker Ladd's book looks at self-concept and self-esteem.

http://www.serve.com/shea/stereodf.htm - **The Meaning and Significance of Stereotypes in Popular Culture**
Many people seem to have stereotypical ideas concerning people of other cultures. Robert Shea looks at stereotypes of Americans held by people from other cultures.

http://www.coping.org/seas/model.htm – **Tools for Coping**

CHAPTER 3: Verbal Communication

Learning Objectives

After studying this chapter, you should be able to answer the following questions:

- What is language?
- What is a speech community?
- What is the relationship between language and meaning?
- How does language change?
- How do gendered language differences affect language use?
- How can you increase the clarity of your messages?
- How can you improve your language usage so that it is more specific?
- How can you use the skills of dating and indexing generalizations to increase the accuracy of your messages?
- How can you phrase messages so that they are perceived as appropriate to the situation?

Interactive Chapter Outline

I. The Nature of Language

_____

_____

    A. Uses of Language

_____

_____

    B. Language and Meaning

_____

_____

    C. Meaning varies across Subgroups in the Speech Community

_____

_____

   D. Cultural Differences in Verbal Communication

_____

_____

   E. Gender differences in Verbal Communication

_____

_____

II. Speaking more clearly

_____

_____

   A. Use Specific Language

_____

_____

   B. Providing Details and Information

_____

_____

   C. Dating Information

_____

D. Indexing Generalizations

III. Speaking Appropriately

A. Adapt Formality to the Situation

B. Limit use of Jargon and Slang

C. Avoid Profanity and Vulgarities

D. Use Inclusive Language

1. _____

2. _____

3. _____

E. Shun Hate Speech

Key Terms

language (p. 52)

speech community (p. 52)

words (p. 52)

denotation (p. 54)

syntactic context (p. 54)

connotation (p. 54)

low-context cultures (p. 55)

high-context cultures (p. 55)

_____

_____

specific language (p. 57)

_____

_____

concrete words (p. 57)

_____

_____

precise words (p. 57)

_____

_____

dating information (p. 60)

_____

_____

generalizing (p. 61)

_____

_____

indexing (p. 61)

_____

_____

speaking appropriately (p. 62)

_____

_____

jargon (p. 63)

_____

slang (p. 63)

generic language (p. 64)

nonparallel language (p. 65)

marking (p. 65)

hate speech (p. 66)

Activity 3.1 Test Your Competence - Clarifying General Statements (p. 60)

Rewrite each statement on the following page to make it more specific. Work to make general and abstract words more concrete and precise. Add details and examples. You can complete this activity on the Communicate! web site.

1. My neighbor has a lot of animals that she keeps in her yard.

2. When I was a little girl, we lived in a big house in the Midwest.

3. My husband works for a large newspaper.

4. She got up late and had to rush to get to school. But she was late anyway.

5. Where'd you find that thing?

6. I really liked going to that concert. The music was great.

7. I really respect her.

8. My boyfriend has long hair and a tattoo.

9. She was wearing a colorful scarf and bright shirt that was a little short.

10. We need to have more freedom to choose our courses.

Activity 3.2 Test Your Competence - Dating & Indexing Messages (p. 62)
Rewrite each of the messages below so that they are dated and/or indexed. You
can also complete this activity on the Communicate! web site

1. Oh, Jamie's an accounting major so I'm sure that she keeps her checkbook
balanced.

2. Forget taking statistics, it's an impossible course.

3. Never try talking to Jim in the morning, he's always grouchy.

4. Don't bother to buy that book for class. You'll never use it.

5. I can't believe you bought a dog. I mean, all they do is shed.

Observe and Analyze Activity 3.3 Observe and Analyze: Crude Language Audit (p. 64)
For the next three days, keep a log of each incident where you use crude or vulgar
language or hate speech. Record where you were, who you were with, what you said,
and why you choose to use the language you did. At the end of the three days review
and analyze your data. Based on your analysis write a paragraph in the space below
that describes your crude language behavior. How pervasive is your use of crude
speech? Are there particular settings or certain people you are more likely to swear in
front to? Are there settings or with people you are less likely to swear? What words are
your "favorites." Why do you use crude speech? Then evaluate how satisfied you are
with the frequency with which you use vulgar language and with your reasons for using
crude speech. Do you think that you are more crude and vulgar in your speech
practices today or has your use of crude language improved. To what do you attribute
any change. You can download additional log sheets at the Communicate! web site.

Crude Language Audit Log Sheet for Activity 3.3

Date and aprx time	Setting	Others present	Crude language	Reason for language

Activity 3.4 – Denotative Meanings

1. Compile a list of ten slang or "in" words. Discuss how the meanings you assign to these words differ from the meanings your parents or grandparents assign to them (for example, "He's bad!"). Use the worksheet below to complete your work.

Word	Your Meanings	Parents/Grandparents Meanings
1.		
2.		
3.		
4.		
5.		
6.		
7.		
8.		
9.		
10.		

2. Write your own definition of each of the following words; then go to a dictionary and see how closely your definition matches the dictionary's

building_____

_____

justice_____

_____

love_____

_____

success_____

_____

band_____,_____

_____

glass_____

_____

peace_____

_____

freedom_____

_____

honor_____

_____

Activity 3.5 – Synonyms

One good way to increase specificity, concreteness, and precision is to use synonyms. Think of a word, then list words that mean about the same thing. For example, synonyms for "happy" are *glad, joyful*, and *pleased*. When you have completed your list, refer to a book of synonyms, such as *Roget's Thesaurus*, to find other words. Then, using the worksheet that follows, write what you think is the meaning of each word, focusing on the shades of difference in meaning among the words. When you are done, look up each word. The goal of this exercise is to select the best word to express your idea.

Original Word: _____

List of Words with similar meaning and their definitions:

1._____

2._____

3._____

4._____

5._____

Additional words found using a book of synonyms and their definitions:

1._____

2._____

3._____

4._____

5._____

Which word is the most specific, concrete or precise for your intended meaning?

Activity 3.6 – Monitoring Your Use of Language

Tape record at least ten minutes of your conversation with a friend of family member. Talk about a subject that you hold strong views about: affirmative action, welfare, taxes, candidates for office, etc. Be sure to get permission from the other person before you tape. At first, you may feel self-conscious about the recorder. But as you get into the discussion, it is quite likely that you will be able to converse normally.

Next, play back the tape and take notes of sections where your language might have been clearer. Using these notes, write better expressions of your ideas for each section you noted by using more precise, specific, and concrete language and by dating and indexing generalizations.

Now replay the tape again. This time take notes on any racist, sexist, or biased expression that you used. Using these notes, write more appropriate expressions for the ones you used.

Finally, using the worksheet that follows, write a paragraph or two that describes what you have learned about your use of language from this experience.

Monitoring Your Use of Language Worksheet

Conversation time and date: _____

Conversation participants: _____

Conversation topic: _____

Areas of unclear language: _____

_____

_____

Areas of sexist, racist or biased language: _____

_____

_____

What have you learned?

3.7 Using InfoTrac College Edition

Although it is easy to spot sexism in language when someone uses a negative slang term to describe a person of the opposite sex, there are other ways language can be considered "sexist."

Using the InfoTrac College Edition subject guide, enter the search terms "sexism in language." Click on "Periodical references." See "Gender Issues in Advertising Language," Nancy Artz (1999). Focus on one of the issues discussed in the article. What is the significance of the examples presented? Why should people be concerned about this issue?

3.8 Using InfoTrac College Edition

It is interesting to observe how language use and word choice changes over time. Using the InfoTrac College Edition subject guide, attempt to find information on how language use and word choice has changed over time. Be sure to discuss the article "One person's word choice can be another's insult" *Sarasota Herald Tribune*, Dec 9, 2001 pBS3. What are some of the reasons for the changing use of words?

3.9 Using InfoTrac College Edition

Using InfoTrac College Edition, find and read the article "I love you man: Overt expression of affection in male-male interaction," by Mormon and Floyd. Summarize the article using the worksheet below, then develop guidelines for how men can use language to develop intimacy.

Article Summary:

Guidelines for Creating Intimacy Using Language:

3.10 Using Technology

How your ideas are worded can make a great deal of difference in whether people will understand or be influenced by what you say. You can use your word processing software to help you with your brainstorming. Nearly every word processing package has a thesaurus (a list of words and their synonyms) for the user to access. For instance, in the Microsoft Word package, the user can highlight a specific word, click on "Tools," drag down to "Thesaurus," and be presented with synonyms for the word. For practice, select any word that you would like to improve upon and look at the synonym choices available. Then select the choice you believe would be most meaningful. For instance, if you highlighted "difficult" when you clicked on Thesaurus, you would be shown *hard, laborious, arduous,* and *strenuous.* If you wanted more choices, you could then highlight one of these words to see additional choices. If you are trying to make the point that studying can be difficult, you might decide to use *arduous* as the most precise word.

Activity 3.11 Analyzing Language

Analyze a political message (campaign ad, speech, interview, etc.) using the concepts of concreteness, precision and specificity of language. Could the message be more concrete, precise and/or specific? If so how? If so, do you think the language was purposefully less concrete, precise and/or specific than it could have been? Why?

Activity 3.12 What Would You Do? A Question of Ethics (p. 67)

Read the scenario on page 67 of your textbook and then answer the questions that follow in the space below.

Web Resource 3.1 Merriam-Webster Online

An easy way to consult a thesaurus is to access Merriam-Webster's online Collegiate Thesaurus. Use your Communicate! CD-ROM to access Web Resource 3.1 Merriam-

Webster Online at the Communicate! website. Select the chapter resources for Chapter 3, then click on "web resources."

Web Resource 3.2 Slang Dictionary

Slang and jargon are so pervasive that there are special dictionaries devoted to the specialized vocabulary of different communities. To access one maintained by California State University at Pomona, use your Communicate! CD-ROM to access Web Resource 3.2: Slang Dictionary at the Communicate! web site.

Web Resource 3.3 Anti-Swearing Policies

To read an InfoTrac College Edition article about anti-swearing policies at work, use your Communicate! CD-ROM to access Web Resource 3.3: Anti-Swearing Policies at the Communicate! web site.

Web Resource 3.4 Cuss Control

For tips on how to "tame your tongue," use your Communicate! CD-ROM to access Web Resource 3.4: Cuss Control Academy at the Communicate! web site.

Chapter 3 Self Test (answers and page references in Appendix)

True/False

1. The text defines language as the body of symbols and the systems for their use that are common to the people of the same language community.

2. Connotative meanings are the standard dictionary meanings for words.

3. A word's meaning can be affected by other words in the same sentence.

4. Saying "35mm SLR" instead of "camera" is an example of word concreteness.

5. Dating information is telling when the information was true.

6. The Untied States is a speech community

7. One of the uses of language is to talk about language.

Multiple Choice

1. Which of the following is true of denotative meanings?
   a. meanings change over time
   b. meanings vary depending on life experiences
   c. there can be more than one denotative meaning for a word
   d. all of these are true
   e. none of these are true

2. Saying "A professor puts in long, hard years to earn his degree"
   a. is an example of word connotation
   b. is an example of word denotation
   c. may be an example of sexist language
   d. may be an example of specific language

3. One of the best skills to use to avoid stereotyping is
   a. dating
   b. feedback
   c. denotation
   d. connotation
   e. indexing

4. In response to the statement "I don't think we should ask Jessica to be on the team – smart kids make lousy athletes," you might use an indexing response such as
    a. although geniuses are usually weak, we don't know Jessica is a genius
    b. we can still ask her to be on the team because she is our friend
    c. Its true Jessica is smart, but we don't know if she is athletic too.
    d. Jessica is not as smart as you think
    e. None of these are indexing statements

5. Jargon
    a. is technical terminology
    b. is never appropriate
    c. is often useful for dating information
    d. is the same as slang
    e. none of the above

6. A speech community
    a. is a group of people who speak the same language
    b. can range in size from just a few people to hundreds of millions
    c. is the same as a language community
    d. all of the above
    e. none of the above

7. Your friend tells you he will be around to see you "tomorrow morning." He shows up at 11:45am while you expected him at 9am. You and he get into a discussion about the meaning of "tomorrow morning." This is an example of
    a. how we use language to discuss things outside our immediate experience.
    b. indexing
    c. using language to limit
    d. using language to talk about language

8. In a high-context culture,
    a. "Yes" may mean "no."
    b. meaning is presented directly
    c. context is irrelevant
    d. none of the above
    e. all of the above

Essay

1. Discuss the differences between low-context and high-context cultures.

2. Analyze the statement "women tend to use both more intensifiers and more hedges than men."

3. Compare and contrast connotative and denotative language. Provide examples.

4. What are the key aspects of speaking appropriately? Be sure to include an example of each.

5. What are the four uses of language? Provide an example of each.

Helpful Links

http://www.cusscontrol.com – **Cuss Control**
For tips on how to clean up your language, visit Cuss Control.

http://www.apa.udel.edu/apa/publications/texts/nonsexist.html - **Guidelines for Non-Sexist Use of Language**
The language policy of the American Philosophical Association is an excellent example of both the rationale for and implementation of language use guidelines.

http://www.uottawa.ca/academic/arts/writcent/hypergrammar/conndeno.html -
Connotations and Denotations
Written by David Megginson of the University of Ottawa, this site offers a concise look at connotations and offers an example.

http://honolulu.hawaii.edu/intranet/committees/FacDevCom/guidebk/teachtip/inclusiv.htm - **Do's and Don'ts of Inclusive Language**
From the Honolulu County Committee on the Status of Women. A set of guidelines on the use of inclusive language.

http://www.britannica.com/dictionary - Britannica **Dictionary and Thesaurus**
Another good online dictionary and thesaurus.

(See your Communicate! CD-ROM for links to other websites referenced in your text.)

CHAPTER 4: Communicating Through Nonverbal Behavior

Learning Objectives

After studying this chapter, you should be able to answer the following questions:

- What are the differences between verbal and nonverbal communication?
- What types of body motions have communication functions?
- What is paralanguage?
- What are the elements of paralanguage, and how does each affect message meaning?
- How do body type, clothing, poise, touching behavior, and use of time affect self-presentation?
- How is communication affected by the use pf physical space?
- How do temperature, lighting, and color affect communication?
- What are some cultural variations that affect our interpretation of nonverbal communication behaviors?

Interactive Chapter Outline

I. The Nature of Nonverbal Communication Behavior

_____

_____

II. Body Motions

_____

_____

    A. Eye Contact

_____

_____

    B. Facial Expression

_____

_____

C. Gesture

_____

_____

D. Posture

_____

_____

E. How Body Motions are Used

    1. _____

    2. _____

    3. _____

    4. _____

    5. _____

F. Cultural Variations

    1. _____

    2. _____

G. Gender Variations

    1. _____

    2. _____

III. Paralanguage

_____

_____

A. Vocal Characteristics

_____

_____

B. Vocal Interferences

_____

_____

IV. Self-Presentation

_____

_____

A. Body type

_____

_____

B. Clothing and Personal Grooming

_____

_____

C. Poise

_____

_____

D. Touch

_____

E. Time

1. _____

2. _____

3. _____

F. Cultural Variations in Self-Presentation

1. _____

2. _____

V. Managing Your Communication Environment

_____

_____

A. Space

1. _____

2. _____

3. _____

B. Temperature, Lighting and Color

1. _____

2. _____

3. _____

C. Cultural Variations in Environment Management

_____

Key Terms

nonverbal communication behaviors (p.72)

_____

_____

kinesics *or* body motions (p. 73)

_____

_____

eye contact *or* gaze (p. 73)

_____

_____

facial expression (p. 73)

_____

_____

gestures (p. 74)

_____

_____

posture (p. 74)

_____

_____

sign language (p. 74)

_____

_____

paralanguage (p. 77)

_____

_____

pitch (p. 77)

_____

_____

volume (p. 77)

_____

_____

rate (p. 77)

_____

_____

quality (p. 77)

_____

_____

vocal interferences (p. 77)

_____

_____

poise (p. 81)

_____

_____

touch or haptics (p. 81)

_____

_____

duration (p. 82)

_____

_____

activity (p. 82)

_____

_____

punctuality (p. 82)

_____

_____

territory (p. 87)

_____

_____

Exercises

Skill Learning Activity 4.1 Observe and Analyze: Body Motions (p. 76)

Find a public setting (for example, a restaurant) where you can observe two people having a conversation. They should be close enough to you so that you can observe their eye contact, facial expression, and gesture—but not close enough that you can hear what they are saying. Carefully observe the interaction with the goal of answering the following questions: What is their relationship? How did each person feel about the conversation. Did feelings change over the course of the conversation? Was one person more dominant? What seemed to be the nature of the conversation (social chit-chat, plan making, problem solving, argument, intimate discussion)? Take notes of the specific nonverbal behavior that led you to each conclusion and write a paragraph describing this experience and what you have learned.

Activity 4.1 Observation Form: Body Motions
Behavior (frequency)

	Participant 1			Participant 2		
Eye contact	High	Med	Low	High	Med	Low
Smiling	High	Med	Low	High	Med	Low
Forward lean of body	High	Med	Low	High	Med	Low
Touches or plays with hair	High	Med	Low	High	Med	Low
Touches or plays with clothes	High	Med	Low	High	Med	Low
Taps hand or fingers on surface	High	Med	Low	High	Med	Low
Arm position relative to body	High	Med	Low	High	Med	Low

What is their relationship?

☐ Acquaintances ☐ Intimate friends ☐ Romantic partners

☐ Business associates ☐ Friends

What type of conversation did this appear to be?

☐ Social chit-chat ☐ Plan making ☐ Problem solving

☐ Argument ☐ Intimate sharing

How did each person feel about the conversation (what emotions were displayed)?

Participant 1:

Participant 2:

Did feelings change over the course of the discussion? If so, how?

Participant 1:

Participant 2:

Who was more dominant?

☐ Participant 1

☐ Participant 2

☐ Neither seemed to dominate

Activity 4.2 Observe and Analyze: Self-Presentation Audit (p. 83)
Once you have completed the audit sheet below, review how you have described yourself on each of the self-presentation dimensions. Then write a short essay in which you describe how you present yourself, evaluate how satisfied you are with this image, and list what if any adjustments to your self-presentation you would like to make so that your self-presentation matches the image you are trying to project.

Self-Presentation Audit

1. Body type

   a. What is your body type?

   b. How does your body type affect your communication with others?

   c. Given your body type, are you in "good shape."

   d. Does your body type seem to affect how others react to you?

2. Clothing and personal grooming

   a. Take a tour of your closet and drawers. Describe your dominant clothing style.

   b. Why do you choose to dress as you do?

   c. What does your style of dress communicate to those who see you?

   d. Is this consistent with the image you wish to project?

   e. To what extent do the clothes you own permit you to alter your image?

   f. Are there certain types of clothing that you feel you should acquire in order to project a different image? If so, describe the clothing and how it would alter the image you project.

g. Do you have any body art (permanent tattoos)? If so, describe the location(s) and design(s).

h. How did you choose the location(s) for the body art?

i. If you have body art that is usually visible, what did you want those who saw it to think about you? What do you think those who see the tattoo think about you? Are you pleased that they would conclude this?

j. Do you have body piercing? If so, describe the locations and the jewelry that you usually wear in them.

k. How did you choose the location(s)?

l. If you have piercings that are usually visible, what did you want those who saw them to think about you? What do you think those who see the piercings think? Are you pleased that they would conclude this?

3. Poise

a. How comfortable are you when you meet strangers?

b. How comfortable are you in expressing your ideas in a small gathering of friends?

c. How well are you able to figure out what

must be done and to take charge in a crisis?

d. Do you enjoy speaking in front of a large group of people?

e. Do you enjoy the job interviewing process and find it easy to answer questions and present your ideas?

f. Are you satisfied with your level of poise?

g. Do others praise you for your self-confidence?

4. Touch

a. Do you like to touch others?

b. Are you comfortable being touched by others?

c. Are you comfortable giving a stranger a firm hand shake?

d. Are you comfortable hugging a casual acquaintance?

e. Do you find it easy to initiate hugging?

f. Do you touch more or less than others in your family? Friendship circle? Workplace?

g. Have other people commented on your use of touch? If so, what have they said?

h. Overall, what messages do you think you send to others by how you use touch?

i. Are you satisfied with these messages?

5. Time

a. How well do your expectations for the duration of activities meet the realities that you encounter? Do you consistently over- or underestimate the time that activities will last? How does this affect others perceptions of and communication with you?

_____
_____
_____
_____
_____
_____
_____

b. Do your activities correspond to those expected in a given period, or do you keep a personal schedule that is at odds with the expectations of most of the other people with whom you interact? How does your activity schedule affect what others think about you?

_____
_____
_____
_____
_____
_____
_____

c. How do you view time? Are you more of monochronic or a polychronic in your use of time? Do you usually arrive Very early? Early? Exactly on time? Late? Very late? Do others comment on your early or late arrival? How does this affect how others see you?

_____
_____
_____
_____
_____
_____

d. How well does your use of time correspond to that of those with whom you communicate most frequently?

_____
_____
_____

Activity 4.3 Observe & Analyze - Violating Intimate Space Norms (p. 88)
Enter a crowded elevator. Get on it and face the back. Make direct
eye contact with the person you are standing in front of. When you disembark record
the person's reactions. On the return trip, introduce yourself to the person who is
standing next to you and engage in an animated conversation. Record the reaction of
the person and others around you. Get on an empty elevator and stand in the exact
center. Do not move when others board. Record their reactions. Be prepared to share
what you have observed with your classmates.

Activity 4.4 – Gender Variations in Body Motions
Find a place in the cafeteria or another public spot where you can observe the conversation of others. You are to observe the nonverbal behaviors of three dyads for at least five minutes each. First, observe the interaction of two men, then the interaction of two women, and finally, the interaction of a man and a woman. Using the Observation Tally Sheet provided here, record each participant's behavior and any other behavioral cues you note. Using these observation notes, review the material on male and female use of body motions. Did your observations confirm these trends? If they did not, develop an explanation about why they didn't, using the sheet that follows.

Nonverbal Behavior Observation Form: Body Motions

Dyad #1:

Behavior (frequency)	Participant 1 (sex:)			Participant 2 (sex:)		
Eye contact	High	Med	Low	High	Med	Low
Smiling	High	Med	Low	High	Med	Low
Forward lean of body	High	Med	Low	High	Med	Low
Touches or plays with hair	High	Med	Low	High	Med	Low
Touches or plays with clothes	High	Med	Low	High	Med	Low
Taps hand or fingers on surface	High	Med	Low	High	Med	Low
Arm position relative to body	High	Med	Low	High	Med	Low

Dyad #2:

Behavior (frequency)	Participant 1 (sex:)			Participant 2 (sex:)		
Eye contact	High	Med	Low	High	Med	Low
Smiling	High	Med	Low	High	Med	Low
Forward lean of body	High	Med	Low	High	Med	Low
Touches or plays with hair	High	Med	Low	High	Med	Low
Touches or plays with clothes	High	Med	Low	High	Med	Low
Taps hand or fingers on surface	High	Med	Low	High	Med	Low
Arm position relative to body	High	Med	Low	High	Med	Low

Dyad #3:

Behavior (frequency)	Participant 1 (sex:)			Participant 2 (sex:)		
Eye contact	High	Med	Low	High	Med	Low

Smiling	High	Med	Low	High	Med	Low
Forward lean of body	High	Med	Low	High	Med	Low
Touches or plays with hair	High	Med	Low	High	Med	Low
Touches or plays with clothes	High	Med	Low	High	Med	Low
Taps hand or fingers on surface	High	Med	Low	High	Med	Low
Arm position relative to body	High	Med	Low	High	Med	Low

Using these observation notes, review the material on male and female use of body motions. Did your observations confirm these trends? If they did not, develop an explanation about why they didn't:

Activity 4.5 – Vocal Interferences

Tape record yourself talking for several minutes about any subject. When you finish, estimate the number of vocal interferences you used. Then replay the tape and compare the actual number with your estimate. How close was your estimate? Wait a day or two and try it again. As your ear becomes trained, your estimates will be closer to the actual number. Keep a record of your improvement suing the worksheet provided below. Now that you have raised your awareness, identify the vocal interference you use most frequently and develop a communication improvement plan (see sample in Chapter 1) to reduce your use of that vocal interference.

Vocal Interference Worksheet

	Date	Estimated Number	Actual Number	Difference
1.				
2.				
3.				
4.				
5.				
6.				
7.				
8.				
9.				
10.				

Most commonly used interference:

<u>Activity 4.6 – Cultural Differences in Self-Presentation</u>
Interview or converse with two international students from different countries. Try to select students whose cultures differ from one another and from the culture with which you are most familiar. Develop a list of questions related to the self-presentation behaviors discussed in your text and record them in the space provided below and on the following page. Try to understand how people in the international student's country differ from you in their use of nonverbal self-presentation behaviors. Prepare to share what you have learned with your classmates.

Interview Questions and Answers (Student #1):

Interview Questions and Answers (Student #2):

4.7 Using InfoTrac College Edition

Touching behavior can be perceived as a sign of comforting, affection, or harassment. Using the InfoTrac College Edition subject guide, enter the term "touch." Click on "periodical references." Then open "Just the right touch," Patrick McCormick (June 1999) for a discussion of touch as comforting. Under what circumstances is touch most comforting?

4.8 Using InfoTrac College Edition

A great deal of research has been done on the importance of touch in healing and health care. Using InfoTrac College Edition, find Studies Give new Meaning to Hands-on Healing, *Psychology Today*, March 2000 v33 i2 p25. Then using the "View other articles linked to these subjects" feature of InfoTrac College Edition, find similar articles and summarize their findings below. Were you surprised at what you found?

4.9 Using Technology (p 81)

As you watch a tape or DVD of a movie or a television program, select a segment where two people are talking with each other for a couple of minutes. The first time you watch, mute the audio (turn off the sound). Based on nonverbal behaviors alone, determine the climate of the conversation (Are the people flirting? In conflict? Discussing an issue? Kidding around? Making small talk?). What nonverbal behaviors and reactions led you that conclusion? Watch the video a second time, observing nonverbals but also listening to vocal variations in volume, pitch, and rate of speed. Do any of these vocal cues add to your assessment? Then watch it a third time, focusing on what the characters are saying. Now analyze the segment. What percentage of meaning came from nonverbal elements? What did you learn from this exercise?

4.9 Using the Internet

Using e-mail, chat room, discussion board or online instant messaging software, conduct a running conversation with a friend, classmate or other acquaintance. Do not use videoconferencing software. Be sure to discuss several issues, engaging in both serious and humorous interactions. Analyze the conversation and its outcomes. Were there any ambiguities or misunderstandings? Were there any moments when you could not tell if your partner was being funny, serious, sarcastic, or emotional? Were there any times when your partner could not tell your level of sarcasm, humor, or emotion? Were these problems resolved? If so, how? Would a face-to-face conversation have avoided some or all of these problems? Why?

4.10 What Would You Do? (p. 89)
Read the *What Would You Do: A Question of Ethics* scenario on page 89 of your text.
Answer the following questions in the space provided here.

1. Analyze Barry's nonverbal behavior. What was he attempting to achieve?

2. How do you interpret Lisa's and Marquez's nonverbal reactions to Barry?

3. Was Barry's behavior ethically acceptable? Explain.

Web Resource 4.1: Maria Brazil (p. 76)
Use your Communicate! CD-ROM to access Maria Brazil, a U.S. based web site
dedicated to Brazilian Culture. Read about Brazilian body language by clicking on
"Cross Cultural" and clicking on "Brazilian Body Language."

Web Resource 4.2: Welcoming dining rooms (p. 84)
To understand more about the design considerations in planning a welcoming dining room, use your Communicate! CD-ROM to access Web Resource 4.2.

Chapter 4 Self Test (answers and page references in Appendix)

True/False

1. Nonverbal cues provide very little social meaning in interpersonal communication.

2. When Shari uses her hands to show shape and size while saying "A bocce ball is about 6 inches in diameter," she is using body action as an illustrator.

3. When we know we want to be at a job interview on time, we are operating under the aspect of time management known as activity.

4. A person who sits in the same chair every class period illustrates territoriality.

5. In some cultures, eye contact is considered rude.

6. Paralanguage is the nonverbal "sound" of what we hear; how something is said.

7. Asian cultures are for the most part high-contact cultures.

Multiple Choice

1. Pitch
   a. is defined as highness or lowness of tone
   b. changes often accompany volume changes
   c. may be higher when someone is expressing nervousness
   d. all of the above

2. If Dwayne pounds his fist on the table while he is telling Diane "Don't bother me right now," we can say Dwayne is
   a. using body movement to mimic emotion
   b. using body movement to describe emotion
   c. using body movement to emphasize speech

     d. none of the above

3. Vocal characteristics
     a. convey no meaning beyond the words themselves
     b. include pitch, volume, rate, and quality
     c. can convey significant meaning
     d. b and c
     e. none of the above

4. Which of the following is an example of "paralanguage"?
     a. pointing at the dog
     b. moving the furniture around to improve communication
     c. saying one word in a sentence louder than the others
     d. ignoring the dog

5. You are driving a nail with a hammer. You accidentally hit your finger. The look on your face in response to the hammer hitting your thumb would be
     a. a display of the feelings
     b. an adapter to the situation
     c. a tension reliever
     d. a regulator
     e. a polychromic

6. Eye contact
     a. shows we are paying attention
     b. can reveal emotions
     c. allows us to monitor the effects of communication
     d. all of the above

7. We observe Gracie slamming her purse down on the table and loudly yelling "I can't stand calculus!" We then assume that she meant to do this. This is an example of what principle of nonverbal communication?
     a. nonverbal communication accompanies verbal communication
     b. nonverbal communication takes the place of verbal communication
     c. nonverbal communication has less meaning than verbal messages
     d. nonverbal communication is assumed to be intentional by the observer.

8. Body motions
     a. take the place of a word or phrase
     b. illustrate what the speaker is saying
     c. control or regulate the flow of information

      d. relieve tension
      e. all of the above

Essay

1. Discuss some cultural variations in self-presentation

2. Discuss how vocal interferences can influence the perception you make on others.

3. Describe the four distances of informal space found in Hall's research. Give an example of when each would be appropriate.

4. What are the elements of paralanguage, and how does each element affect message meaning? Provide examples to illustrate your points.

5. Discuss why effective communicators need to understand cultural and gender differences in the interpretation of nonverbal behaviors.

Helpful Links

http://www.unl.edu/casetudy/456/traci.htm - **"Analysis of Cultural Communication and Proxemics,"** (By Traci Olsen.)

http://www.csun.edu/~vcecn006/nonverb.html - **"Nonverbal Communication Helps Us Live"**
A helpful review of the importance of nonverbal communication in everyday life. From California State University Northridge.

http://www.ivillage.com/home/fengshui/articles/0,,415228_270596,00.html - **4 Feng Shui Success Stories**
The art of "Feng Shui" is explained in this alternative look at the importance of management of the environment. From iVillage.com.

http://members.aol.com/nonverbal3/eyecon.htm - **Eye Contact**
This site that looks at eye contact from a variety of different perspectives, some with photos for examples. From the Center for Nonverbal Studies

http://members.aol.com/nonverbal2/index.htm - **The Center for Nonverbal Studies homepage** (Created by David Givens.)

(See your Communicate! CD-ROM for links to other websites referenced in your text.)

II

INTERPERSONAL COMMUNICATION

CHAPTER 5: Holding Effective Conversations

Learning Objectives

After studying this chapter, you should be able to answer the following questions:

- What is a conversation?
- How does a casual social conversation differ from a pragmatic problem-consideration conversation?
- What are conversational rules, and what are their distinguishing features?
- What is the cooperative principle?
- How do the maxims of the cooperative principle apply to conversation?
- What skills are associated with effective conversations?
- What guidelines regulate turn-taking behavior?
- What is conversational coherence, and how can it be achieved?
- Why is politeness important in conversation?
- What additional skills are important for electronically mediated communication?

Interactive Chapter Outline

I. Characteristics of Conversation

_____

_____

   A. Casual social conversation

_____

_____

   B. Pragmatic problem consideration conversation

_____

_____

   C. Rules of Conversation

_____

_____

D. Effective Conversation Follows the Cooperative Principle

_____

_____

    1. Quality Maxim _____

    2. Quantity Maxim _____

    3. Relevancy Maxim _____

    4. Manner Maxim _____

    5. Morality Maxim _____

    6. Politeness Maxim _____

II. Guidelines for Effective Conversationalists

_____

_____

A. Prepare to Contribute Interesting Information

    1. _____

    2. _____

    3. _____

B. Ask Questions that Motivate Others to Respond

_____

_____

C. Provide Free Information

_____

_____

D. Practice Appropriate Turn-Taking

_____

_____

1. _____

2. _____

3. _____

4. _____

5. _____

F. Maintain Conversational Coherence

_____

_____

G. Practice Politeness

_____

_____

1. _____

2. _____

3. _____

III. Electronically Mediated Conversations

_____

_____

A. Cell Phones and Electronic Messaging

_____

_____

B. E-Mail

_____

_____

1. _____

2. _____

3. _____

4. _____

5. _____

C. Conversing via Newsgroups and Internet Chat

_____

_____

IV. Cultural Variations in Effective Conversation

_____

Key Terms

conversation (p. 96)

_____

_____

casual social conversations (p. 96)

_____

_____

pragmatic problem-consideration conversations (p. 98)

_____

_____

conversational rules (p. 100)

_____

_____

cooperative principle (p. 101)

_____

_____

maxims (p. 101)

_____

_____

quality maxim (p. 101)

_____

_____

quantity maxim (p. 101)

_____

_____

relevancy maxim (p. 101)

_____

_____

manner maxim (p. 101)

_____

_____

morality maxim (p. 101)

_____

_____

politeness maxim (p. 101)

_____

_____

free information (p. 105)

_____

_____

politeness (p. 107)

_____

_____

positive face needs (p.107)

_____

_____

negative face needs (p. 108)

_____

newsgroup (p. 113)

Internet chat (p. 113)

instant messaging (p. 113)

lurking (p. 113)

flaming (p. 113)

netiquette (p. 114)

FAQs (p. 114)

Exercises

Activity 5.1 Observe and Analyze: Following the Cooperative Principle (p. 101-102)

For the next three days keep a log of two or three conversations you have had. After you complete each conversation, take a few moments to record your observations and perceptions. At the end of the three days, analyze your log. Then write a paragraph in which you answer the following questions. How well did I adhere to the maxims of the cooperative principles? Did the extent to which I and my conversational partners adhered to these maxims affect my satisfaction with the conversation? Is there a particular maxim that is more difficult for me to follow? Use the log sheet below or download additional copies using your Communicate! CD-ROM.

Conversation Log (Cooperative Principle)

Day and time	Name(s) of partner(s)	Quality of information	Quantity of information	Relevancy	Manner (thoughts organized)	Morality	Politeness	Overall satisfaction
		/	/	/	/	/	/	/
		/	/	/	/	/	/	/
		/	/	/	/	/	/	/
		/	/	/	/	/	/	/
		/	/	/	/	/	/	/
		/	/	/	/	/	/	/
		/	/	/	/	/	/	/
		/	/	/	/	/	/	/
		/	/	/	/	/	/	/
		/	/	/	/	/	/	/
		/	/	/	/	/	/	/
		/	/	/	/	/	/	/
		/	/	/	/	/	/	/
		/	/	/	/	/	/	/
		/	/	/	/	/	/	/
		/	/	/	/	/	/	/
		/	/	/	/	/	/	/
		/	/	/	/	/	/	/
		/	/	/	/	/	/	/
		/	/	/	/	/	/	/

Activity 5.2 Observe and Analyze: Developing Topics for Conversation (p.105)
Sometimes we have trouble initiating conversations because we can't think of anything to talk about. The goal of this activity is to help you identify topics that you know something about and would enjoy talking about. For each of the categories below, list at least three specific discussions you could initiate.
Current events:
Recent movies:
Recent cultural events in the community:
Recent books I have read:
Recent concerts or plays I have seen:
Hobbies I enjoy:
Recent vacations:
My favorite class:
Now, during the next three days, intentionally introduce some of these subjects into your conversations. How well are you able to develop and sustain conversations on these topics? Did you find these conversations to be more or less satisfying than ones you usually have? Why?

Conversation Topic Log

Conversational category	Topic 1	Topic 2	Topic 3
Current events			
Recent movies			
Recent cultural events in the community			
Recent books I've read			
Recent concerts or plays I've seen			
Hobbies I enjoy			
Recent Vacations			
My favorite class			

Activity 5.3 Test Your Competence - Practicing Politeness (p. 109)
Rephrase each of the face threatening statements below using some form of
positive or negative politeness. To get you started, the authors' model answer is
provided for the first statement. You can complete this activity on line at the
Communicate! web site and compare our responses to the models provided by the
authors. Select the student resources for chapter 5, then click on "Activities."

1. "Tommy, turn down your stereo, you're playing that music too loud."
   Positive Politeness: "Tommy, I'd really appreciate it if you could turn the stereo
   down. I have trouble listening to music when it's this loud."

   Negative Politeness: "Tommy, I know it's your room and you have every right to
   play your music as loud as you want, but could you turn it down a bit, I've got a
   splitting headache."

2. "Lisa, you need to finish your part of the paper so I can get it typed before the
   weekend.

3. "I disagree with what you just said."

4. "Can you stop on your way home and pick up some milk and bread?"

5. "I don't want to see that movie."

7. "I think we should stop seeing each other."

Activity 5.4 Observe & Analyze - Email Audit (p. 113)
For the next week, do not delete any email you receive (except spam), and keep a
copy of all the email you send in a "sent mail" folder. At the end of the week, classify
each message that you have received and written into one of the following
categories: social messages to friends, work-related messages, school related

messages to faculty or other students, inquiries to web sites, or Other. How many messages did you receive each day? What percentage of your messages fell into each category? What percentage of those do you reply to? Write a paragraph describing your email patterns.

Activity 5.5 Conversation Analysis: Susan and Sarah (p.116-118)
Use your Communicate! CD-ROM to access the video clip of Susan & Sarah's conversation. Click on the "In Action" feature, and then select "Susan and Sarah." As you watch the video clip, notice to what extent each of them follow the six conversational maxims. How does each exemplify the guidelines for effective conversationalists? Printed below is a transcript of the conversation. Use the other column to take notes as you watch. Then complete Activity 5.5 online at the Communicate! web site. Select Student Resources for Ch. 5. Click on Skill Activities. After entering your analysis, submit your answer and compare them to the model provided by the authors.
Note: Susan and Sarah are close friends who share the same religious background and the occasional frustrations that their family beliefs cause.

Conversation   Analysis

Susan: So how are you and Bill getting along these days?

Sarah: Oh, not too well, Suze. I think we've got to end the relationships. There are so many issues between us that I just don't have the same feelings.

Susan: Yeah, you know, I could tell. Is there one specific thing that's a problem?

Sarah: And it's ironic because early on I didn't think it would be problem, but it is. You know, he's not Jewish and since we've started talking about marriage, I've realized that it is a problem. While Bill's a great guy, our backgrounds and beliefs just don't mesh.

I never realized how important my Jewishness was to me until I was faced with converting. And Bill feels similarly about it.

Susan: I think I'm kind of lucky, well, in the long run. Remember in high school my parents wouldn't let me go out with anybody who wasn't Jewish? At the time I resented that and we both thought they were reactionary, but now I'm kind of glad. At the time my parents said, "you never know what's going to come out of a high-school relationship." Well, they never got that far, but it did force me to think about things.

Sarah: Yes, I remember that. You hated it. It's amazing to realize your parents can actually be right about something?

Susan: Right, it was the pits at the time, but at least it spared me the pain you and Bill are going through. It must be awful to be in love with someone that you realize you don't wasn't as a life partner.

Sarah: Exactly, but I'm glad that my parents didn't restrict my dating to Jewish guys. I've learned a lot by dating a variety of people and I know that I've made this decision independently. Bill's a great guy, but for me to be me, I need to partner with a Jewish man—and Bill knows he can't be that. Making this choice has been hard, but it's helped me to grow. I guess I understand myself better.

Susan: So where have you guys left it? Are you going to still see each other? Be friends?

Sarah: We hope so. But right now, it's too fresh. It hurts to see him, so we're trying to give each other some space. I uses it will really be tough when I hear he's seeing someone else. But I'll get by.

Susan: Well you know I'm here for you. And

when you're ready there are some really hotties at Hillel. I'll be glad to introduce you.

Sarah: Thanks Suze. So how's your new job?

Susan: Oh, it's great. I really like my boss and I've gotten a new assignment that fits right in with my major. Plus my boss has flexible in assigning my hours. I just wish that It wasn't so far away.

Sarah: I thought it was downtown.

Susan: It is, it takes me over an hour because I have to change buses three times.

Sarah: Wow—are you at least able to study while you ride?

Susan: Not really. I get carsick.

Sarah: Oh I forgot. Bummer.

Susan: Yeah but I'll survive. Listen, I hate to leave, but I've got a class in 10 minutes and if we're late the professor glares when we walk in. I don't need that.

Sarah: What a jerk.

Susan: Yeah, well I've got to run.

Sarah: Same time tomorrow?

Susan: Sure.

Activity 5.6 – Using Politeness

Think about the last time you committed a face-threatening act (FTA). Try to reconstruct the situation. What did you say? – try to recall as specifically as possible the exact words you used.

Analyze your FTA in terms of familiarity and status, power, and risk. Did you have greater or lesser status? Did you have greater or lesser social power? Was the risk of hurting the person large or small? In light of you analysis, write three different ways that you could have made your request. Try one that uses positive face statement; try one that uses negative face statements; try one that combines positive and negative statements. Record your observations and analysis below. Record your three different requests on the following section.

Journal Activity 5.6 (three statements)
Positive Face Statement:

Negative Face Statement:

Combined Positive and Negative Statement:

5.7 Using InfoTrac College Edition

Certainly one important aspect of politeness is courtesy. Using InfoTrac College Edition, under the subject "courtesy," find "The case for courtesy in business writing," *Everett Business Journal*, Oct 2003 v6 i10 pB11(1). Do you think courtesy matters? To what extent? Find other articles to support your argument.

5.8 Using InfoTrac College Edition

Research the subject "cell phone etiquette. Find several articles that address the topic and summarize their findings below. Were you surprised with any of the findings?

5.9 Using Technology

Think of times that you've made a call outside your home using a wireless cell telephone. How do your conversations differ from those you have made on a wired phone? Are they longer? Shorter? More focused on pragmatic problem considerations than on casual social exchanges? Why do you think this is true? What differences do you see in the etiquette of the way you handle such conversations in comparison to the way you would handle them if you were face to face?

Activity 5.10 What Would You Do? A Question of Ethics (p. 118-119)

Read the *What Would You Do: A Question of Ethics* scenario on page 118 of your text. Answer the following questions in the space provided here.

1. Have you ever talked with someone like John? Where did John go wrong in his conversational skills? What should he have done differently?

2. What are the ethical implications of Louisa and the rest of the group sneaking out the side door without saying anything to John? Defend your position.

Web Resource 5.1: Cell Phone Etiquette (p. 111)
Check out the "ten commandments" of cell phone etiquette by using your Communicate! CD-ROM to access Web Resource 5.2: Cell Phone Etiquette.

Web Resource 5.2: Emoticons (p. 112)
For a listing of the various ways you can express nonverbal emotions online, use your Communicate! CD-ROM to access Web Resource 5.2: Emoticons.

Web Resource 5.3: Email Etiquette (p. 113)
For additional guidelines on the effective use of email, use your Communicate! CD-ROM to access Web Resource 5.3: Email Etiquette.

Web Resource 5.4: Instant Messaging (p. 114)
To learn more about the pros and cons of instant messaging, read "Instant Messaging, Pressuring Teens, Spreading Good and Bad Information" by Jake Wagman, available through InfoTrac College Edition. Use your Communicate! CD-ROM to access Web Resource 5.4: Instant Messaging.

Chapter 5 Self Test (answers and page references in Appendix)

True/False

1. Online conversations are essentially the same as face-to-face conversations.

2. A newsgroup is defined as an online interactive message exchange between two or more people.

3. Lurking is a violation of Netiquette.

4. Maxims are conversational rules of conduct.

5. One characteristic of rules is that are contextual –that they can apply in some situations but not others.

6. While at dinner together, Miguel and Amanda chat about a wide variety of topics designed to meet their needs and build their relationship. This is an example of pragmatic problem-consideration conversation.

7. Tara asks Leon about his vacation to Florida went. Leon replies "ok." This would be a violation of the quantity maxim.

8. Negative face needs is the desire to be free from imposition or intrusion.

Multiple Choice

1. Social conversations differ from problem-consideration conversations in
    a. the kinds of topics discussed
    b. the goals of the conversation
    c. when the conversations occur
    d. all of the above

2. Cindy is talking to her friend Zack about classes for the next semester. She says "I think I'm going to take that Political Communication class in the fall. Jenny told me about and said it would be a good course." This is an example of:
    a. providing turn-taking cues
    b. the manner maxim
    c. quality maxim
    d. prescriptive rules
    e. none of the above

3. Saying to your professor "I can see that you're really busy right now, but I was wondering if you could answer a quick question" is an example of
    a. meeting someone's negative face needs
    b. meeting someone's positive face needs
    c. making a face-threatening act
    d. applied turn-taking rules

4. Face-threatening acts
    a. should be avoided at all times
    b. are common
    c. can be used with positive politeness
    d. both b and c

5. Conversational rules
    a. are prescriptive in nature
    b. can tell us what to do or not to do in a situation
    c. allow for choice in behavior
    d. can vary from situation to situation
    e. all of the above

6. Ralph asks Richie how to use the new online registration system. Richie explains the process step by step and in order.
    Richie's explanation follows the
    a. quality maxim

b. quantity maxim
c. relevancy maxim
d. manner maxim

7. Lana and Virginia are having a conversation. Lana notices she is talking much more often than Virginia. She makes an effort to speak less often and allow Virginia to speak more. Lana is attempting to:
    a. practice appropriate turn-taking
    b. use the manner maxim
    c. use the rule maxim
    d. none of the above

8. Jeff receives an e-mail from Neil. Jeff spends a little time pondering a reply. After he types his response, he re-reads it, corrects a few typos, and changes a few thoughts. Jeff has taken advantage of what characteristic of e-mail?
    a. delayed feedback
    b. instant messages
    c. netiquette
    d. nonverbal cues

Essay

1. How can one be prepared to contribute interesting information to a conversation?

2. Describe why meaningful questions posed by an initiator should require more than a "yes" or "no" answer.

3. Discuss the techniques for practicing appropriate turn-taking. Give examples of each.

4. Discuss the advantages and disadvantages of e-mail versus a face-to-face interaction.

5. How can "free information" make conversations more interesting and informative? Provide examples.

Helpful Links

http://www.google.com - **Google.com**
The Google Internet search engine is one of the most popular web destinations. Use it to search for information on any topic using a simple search engine.

http://www.dogpile.com – **Dogpile.com**
The Dogpile search engine actually searches a list of other search engines for the topic or key words desired and returns results sorted by the search engine used. Also has white and yellow pages.

http://www.hyperlexia.org/aha_about_conversation.html - **Learning about conversation**
From the Center for Speech and Language Disorders, this site discusses rules of conversation as applied to children with learning and socializing disabilities.

http://www.albion.com/netiquette/ - **Netiquette home page**
"Netiquette" is a set of rules of behavior for electronically mediated communication. From Albion.com.

http://www.executiveplanet.com/ - **International Business Culture, Customs and Etiquette**
Comprehensive site organized by country. Excellent resource provided by Executive Planet.com.

(See your Communicate! CD-ROM for links to other websites referenced in your text.)

CHAPTER 6: Listening and Responding

Learning Objectives

After studying this chapter, you should be able to answer the following questions:

- What five processes are used during listening?
- How can you focus your attention?
- How can you increase your understanding?
- What is empathy?
- How can questioning increase understanding?
- What is paraphrasing?
- What are three tactics that can help you remember what you hear?
- How can you evaluate what you've heard?
- What characterizes support messages?
- What specific verbal messages provide comfort?

Interactive Chapter Outline

I. Attending _____

_____

    1. _____

    2. _____

    3. _____

II. Understanding

_____

_____

    A. Empathy

_____

_____

    1. _____

    2. _____

    3. _____

B. Questioning

_____

_____

    1. _____

    2. _____

    3. _____

    4. _____

C. Paraphrasing

_____

_____

III. Remembering (Retaining Information)

_____

_____

A. Repeat information

_____

_____

B. Construct Mnemonics

_____

_____

C. Take Notes

_____

_____

IV. Critical Analysis

_____

_____

    1. _____

    2. _____

V. Responding Supportively to give Comfort

_____

_____

A. Characteristics of Effective and Ineffective Emotional Support Messages

    1. _____

    2. _____

    3. _____

    4. _____

    5. _____

    6. _____

    7. _____

    8. _____

B. Supporting Positive Feelings

_____

_____

C. Giving Comfort

_____

_____

    1. _____

    2. _____

    3. _____

    4. _____

    5. _____

D. Gender and Cultural Considerations in Comforting

_____

_____

    1. _____

    2. _____

    3. _____

    4. _____

    5. _____

Key Terms

listening (p. 124)

_____

_____

attending (p. 124)

_____

_____

understanding (p. 125)

_____

_____

empathy (p. 125)

_____

_____

empathic responsiveness (p. 125)

_____

_____

perspective taking (p. 126)

_____

_____

sympathetic responsiveness (p. 126)

_____

_____

respect (p. 126)

_____

_____

question (p. 127)

_____

paraphrasing (p. 128)

content paraphrase (p. 128)

feelings paraphrase (p. 128)

remembering (p. 130)

mnemonic device (p. 130)

critical analysis (p. 133)

factual statements (p. 133)

inferences (p. 133)

comfort (p. 134)

supportive messages (p. 136)

clarify supportive intentions (p. 138)

buffering (p. 138)

other-centered messages (p. 139)

reframing (p. 139)

giving advice (p. 140)

Exercises

Skill Learning Activity 6.1 – Empathizing Effectively (p. 127)
Write a paragraph describing a time when you effectively empathized with another person. What was the person's emotional state? How did you recognize it? What were the nonverbal cues? Verbal cues? What type of relationship do you have with this person? How similar at the two of you? What type of empathizing did you use? Why?

Skill Learning Activity 6.2 Test Your Competence - Questions And Paraphrases (p. 129)
Provide an appropriate question and paraphrase for each of the statements below. You can also complete this activity online at the Communicate! web site and compare your answers to the authors'. Select Student Resources for Ch. 6, then click on Skill Learning Activities.

Example: "It's Dionne's birthday, and I've planned a big evening. Sometimes I think Dionne believes I take her for granted—well, after tonight she'll know I think she's something special!"

Question: "What specific things do you have planned?"

Paraphrase: "If I'm understanding you, you're really proud that you've planned a night that's going to be a lot more elaborate than what Dionne expects on her birthday."

1. **Luis**: "It was just another mind numbing class. I keep thinking one of these days Prof. Romero will get excited about something. He's is a real bore!"

2. **Angie**: "Everyone seems to be raving about the new reality show on Channel 5 last night, but I didn't see it. You know, I don't watch the "boob tube."

3. **Kaelin**: "I don't know if it's me or with Mom, but lately she and I just aren't getting along."

4. **Aileen:** "I've got a report due at work and a paper due in management class. On top of that, it's my sister's birthday, and so far I haven't even had time to get her anything. Tomorrow's going to be a disaster."

Skill Learning Activity 6.3 Test Your Competence - Creating Mnemonics (p. 130)
Mnemonics are useful memory aids. Construct a mnemonic for the five phases of the listening process: attending, understanding, remembering, evaluating, and responding. Record your mnemonic. Tomorrow, while you are getting dressed, see whether you can recall the mnemonic you created. Then see whether you can recall the phases of the Listening process from the cues in your mnemonic. How well did you do? Write a brief paragraph describing your experience. You can also complete this activity online. Select Student Resources for Ch. 6, then click on Skill Learning Activities and select this activity.

Skill Learning Activity 6.4 Test Your Competence – Listening to Remember (p. 132)
At the Communicate! web site you can take a listening test to evaluate how well you remember what you hear, with and without notes. The information presented assumes that you are on your firs day of a new job working in a college department office. You will listen to the directions once and then take a test. This first time, you should not take notes. The second time, as you listen, take notes. Then use these notes to help you answer the questions on the second test. To complete this activity online, use your Communicate! CD-ROM to access Student Resources for chapter 6, then click on Skill Learning Activities and select this activity.

Skill Learning Activity 6.5 Test Your Competence – Evaluating Inferences (p. 134)
For each of the statements below, identify the fact(s), and identify the inference(s). Then, write three specific questions that "test" the validity of the inference. You can also complete this activity on-line at the Communicate! web site and compare your answers to the model supplied by the authors. At the web site select Student Resources for Chapter 6, then select this activity.

Example: The campus walk-in health clinic is understaffed. I stopped by the other day and had to wait two hours to be seen.
Fact: I had to wait two hours to be seen at the walk-in clinic
Inference: The clinic is understaffed.
Questions:
    1. Is one person's experience alone enough to support the inference?
    2. Are there times when there is not a backlog?
    3. Are there other things besides staffing levels which could account for the wait?

1. Christy got a 96% on the first test. She must have crammed all weekend.

2. Kali's pregnant. Just look at how tight her jeans are, she can barely keep them buttoned.

3. You can't get a good job, unless you know someone. Mike searched everywhere for six months before he finally talked to his next-door neighbor who hired him for his construction company.

4. If you want to go to dental school when you graduate, forget it. In the past three years, none of the students from this program who applied, got in.

5. Kids today are growing up too fast. I mean, they carry cell phones and everything.

Skill Learning Activity 6.6 Conversation and Analysis (p. 142-144)
Use your Communicate! CD-ROM to access the video clip of Damien and Chris's conversation. Click on the "In Action!" icon in the menu, then click on "Conversation menu" in the menu bar. Select "Damien and Chris Overview" to watch the video (it takes a minute for the video to load). As you watch the interaction, analyze how well Damien uses the skills of active listening and how well his responses demonstrate effective support and comforting. You can respond to this and other analysis questions by clicking on "Analysis" in the menu bar. When you've answered all of the questions, click "Done" to compare your answers to those provided by the authors. Here is a transcript of this conversation which you can use to take notes as you watch the video.

Note: Damien and Chris work in a small shop selling shirts and gifts. Usually they get along well, but lately Chris has seemed standoffish. Damien decides to talk with Chris to see if anything is wrong. Damien approaches Chris in the break room.

Conversation	Analysis
Damien: Chris, you've been kind of quiet lately, man. What's been going on?	
Chris: Nothing.	
Damien: Come on, man, What's going on?	
Chris: Just life. (shrugs) I'm just kind of down right now.	
Damien: Well, what am I here for? I thought we were friends.	
Chris thinks about it and decides to talk about it.	

it.

Chris: Well, Carl's been on my case the last few weeks.

Damien: Why? Did you do something?

Chris: Oh, he says that I'm sloppy when I restock and i'm not always "polite" to our customers. You know, just 'cuz I don't smile all the time. I mean, what does he want—little Mary Sunshine?

Damien: So you're angry with the boss.

Chris: Yeah, I guess. . . no, no, not so angry, I'm just frustrated. I come in to work every day and I try to do my job and I don't complain. You know, I'm sick and tired of getting stuck back there in the stock room reorganizing everything. It's not like they're paying us big bucks here. And Carl shouldn't expect us to be charming with everybody who walks through that door. I mean, half of the people who walk through that door are, well, they're totally rude and act like jerks.

Damien: Yeah, I feel like you on that. Some of those people shouldn't be allowed out in public. What is Carl saying about how you're dealing with the customers?

Chris: Oh, he just says that I've changed and that I'm not being "nice." I mean, he used to call me his top guy.

Damien: I mean, you know how Carl is. He's a fanatic about customer service. You know how, when we first started, he drilled us about being polite and smiling and being courteous at all times. So maybe when he says "you're not being nice," he just means that you're not doing it all the way you used to. I mean, I've notice a change. I mean, you're just not yourself lately. Is anything going on outside of work?

Chris: You could say that. Sarah and I just bought a house, so money's been a bit tight. Now, she wants to quit her job and start a family, and I'm not sure we can afford it. On top of it all, my kid sister shows up a few weeks ago on our doorstep, pregnant, and now she's living with us, so yeah, it is a bit overwhelming. And I'm a bit worried that Carl's going to fire me.

Damien: Wow, that is a lot of stuff! I can understand why you're down, but did Carl really threaten to fire you?

Chris: No, no, but I'm not perfect and he could use my "attitude" as an excuse to fire me.

Damien: Well, did you think about telling him what's been going on? And maybe, you know, he'll understand and cut you some slack.

Chris: Or he could see that I really have changed and he'd can me.

Damien: Ok, well, just tell me this. Do you like working here?

Chris: Yeah, of course I do.

Damien: OK, well, then, you've just got to tough it out. I mean, you've just got to use the game face on these people. You used to be the best at doing that. So you're just gonna have to get back to being a salesman, and leave everything else behind.

_____

_____

_____

_____

_____

Chris: I guess I never realized how much my problems were affecting my work. I thought Carl was just out to get me, but now you're noticing something too, then maybe I have changed. Thanks. Thanks for talking this out.

_____

_____

_____

Activity 6.7 – Attending

Select an information-oriented program on your public television station. Watch at least fifteen minutes of the show while lounging in a comfortable chair or while stretched out on the floor with music playing on a radio in the background. For the next fifteen minutes, make a conscious effort to use the guidelines for increasing attentiveness. Then contrast your listening behaviors. What differences did you note between the second segment and the first? What were the results of those differences?

Activity 6.8 Using InfoTrac College Edition

Why is listening perceived to be important in so many professions? Which specific listening skills seem to be agreed upon as most important?
Using InfoTrac College Edition, search for the subject of "listening." To answer the questions, open several articles and summarize their findings below. Be sure to include the bibliographic information for each article you discuss.

6.9 Using InfoTrac College Edition

Search using the term "Empathy." Find the article with the very long title: "Emotional care of the patient & family in terminal illness: caring for a dying patient can be very demanding. Pat MacDonald explains how expressing empathy can help patients and their families but being aware of your own emotional needs is equally important." Why is empathy important in health care, especially care of the terminally ill? Do you think you could "understand the world of they dying patient?" Summarize the article below.

Activity 6.10 What would you do? A Question of Ethics (p. 144)
Read the *What Would You Do: A Question of Ethics* scenario on page 144 of your text.
Answer the following questions in the space provided here.

1. How ethical was Janeen's means of dealing with her dilemma of not wanting to talk
on the phone but not wanting to hurt Barbara's feelings?

2. Identify ways in which both Janeen and Barbara could have used better and perhaps
more ethical interpersonal communication skills. Rewrite the scenario incorporating
these changes.

Web Resource 6.1: Listening Inventory (p. 124)
Complete an inventory of your listening skills. Use your Communicate! CD-ROM to access Web Resource 6.1: Listening Inventory.

Web Resource 6.2: Listening and Empathetic Responding (p. 126)
To explore suggestions for developing empathy, use your Communicate! CD-ROM to access Web Resource 6.2: Listening and Empathetic Responding.

Web Resource 6.3: Mnemonics (p.131)
You can read more about mnemonic techniques at MindTools.com. Use your Communicate! CD-ROM to access Web Resource 6.3: Mnemonics.

Chapter 6 Self Test (answers and page references in Appendix)

True/False

1. Questions should be phrased as complete sentences.

2. Listening involves noting verbal cues only.

3. Saying something over three or four times until you remember it is an example of a mnemonic.

4. Inferences are never true.

5. Brant Burleson is a noted scholar in the area of mnemonics.

6. Comforting usually just takes a single phrase or sentence.

7. Offering alternative explanations to help your partner understand a situation in a different way is called reframing.

Multiple Choice

1. "The process of receiving, attending to, and assigning meaning to aural and visual stimuli" is the definition of
    a. listening
    b. critical analysis
    c. empathy
    d. inference making

2. Physical posture
  a. is irrelevant to listening
  b. guarantees successful listening
  c. is part of being prepared both mentally and physically to listen
  d. is only part of assigning meaning to information
  e. none of the above

3. Brad is comforting Daniel because Daniel is upset that Lise has not called him as she promised she would. He assumes Lise no longer likes him. Brad tells Daniel that the mall where Lise works has awful cell phone reception and she simply may not be able to get a signal. Brad's behavior is an example of:
  a. other-centered message
  b. reframing
  c. supporting negative feelings
  d. none of the above

4. Fred says "Man, I really blew that assignment, I guess I'm just not cut out for physics!" Barney replies "If I understand you right, you didn't do a good job on last night's homework?" Barney is using what strategy of improving understanding?
  a. empathy
  b. questioning
  c. attending
  d. paraphrasing
  e. articulating

5. Michelle remembers phone numbers by visualizing how her fingers move across the dial pad, even to the extent of pretending to "dial" a phone number in air. This artificial memory aid is an example of
  a. inference making
  b. a mnemonic device
  c. a selection device
  d. critical analysis
  e. supporting behavior

6. Offering supportive messages
  a. is part of the responding process
  b. can help express care and interest in the other
  c. can cheer up the other
  d. all of the above
  e. none of the above

7. Albert has just told Paco that he just found out he failed his biology midterm. If Paco pictures himself in that same situation, imagines how he would feel in that situation, and then assumes that Albert is feeling the same way, Paco is exemplifying:
   a. respect
   b. framing
   c. perspective taking
   d. questioning

8. Carla just told Keri that Zack broke up with her. Keri feels compassion and concern for her friend, but does not feel Carla's sense of loss and sadness. What best represents Keri's feelings:
   a. She is feeling empathy for Carla
   b. She is feeling sympathy for Carla
   c. She is feeling respect for Carla
   d. She is perspective taking

Essay

1. Describe the different stages of the listening process.

2. Describe several ways to improve your ability to remember information.

3. Explain the difference between factual statements and inferences and discuss why it is important to understand the difference.

4. What are some characteristics of effective support messages? Give examples.

5. What is the difference between sympathy and empathy? Provide an example of each.

Helpful Links

http://www.csbsju.edu/academicadvising/help/eff-list.html - **Effective Listening**
College of Saint Benedict | Saint John's University study skills guide for effective
listening and note-taking in class

http://www.listen.org/quotations/quotes.html - **Quotations About Listening**
The International Listening Association's list of quotes about listening. The
association's home page is http://www.listen.org/.

http://userpages.umbc.edu/~cweide1/oraloutline.html - "**Barriers to Effective
Listening**"
by Jack E. Hulbert.

http://marriage.about.com/cs/listening/index.htm?once=true&iam=dpile&terms=+effectiv
e++listening - **Listening**
This site from About.com explores the importance of listening in marriage.

http://www.vandruff.com/art_converse.html - "**Conversational Terrorism**"
This site includes is a humorous approach to a discussion of what not to do when
responding to others.

http://www.campaign-for-
learning.org.uk/campaigns/learningatwork/lawday/resources/tolerenceskills.htm -
Tolerance & Empathy Skills Resources
The Campaign for Learning's Tolerance and Empathy Skills Resources site.
(See your Communicate! CD-ROM for links to other websites referenced in your text.)

CHAPTER 7: Sharing Personal Information: Self-Disclosure and Feedback

Learning Objectives

After studying this chapter, you should be able to answer the following questions:

- What is self-disclosure?
- What are the guidelines for effective disclosure?
- When and how does one describe feelings?
- What are the differences between displaying feelings and describing feelings?
- What can you do to improve giving praise and constructive criticism?
- What is assertiveness?
- How does assertiveness differ from passive or aggressive behavior?
- How can you assert yourself appropriately?

Interactive Chapter Outline

I. Self-Disclosure

_____

_____

   A. Guidelines for Appropriate Self-Disclosure

_____

_____

      1. _____

      2. _____

      3. _____

      4. _____

      5. _____

B. Cultural and Gender Differences

_____

_____

II. Disclosing Feelings

_____

_____

A. Withholding Feelings

_____

_____

B. Displaying Feelings

_____

_____

C. Describing Feelings

_____

_____

1. _____

2. _____

3. _____

4. _____

5. _____

6. _____

IV. Giving Personal Feedback

_____

_____

A. Describing Behavior

_____

_____

B. Praise

_____

_____

C. Giving Constructive Criticism

_____

_____

1. _____

2. _____

3. _____

4. _____

V. Assertiveness

_____

_____

A. Contrasting Methods of Expressing our Needs and Rights

_____

1. Passive Behavior

_____

_____

2. Aggressive Behavior

_____

_____

3. Assertive Behavior

_____

_____

B. Situations in Which Assertiveness is Appropriate

1. Refusing a request

_____

_____

2. Expressing a preference or right

_____

_____

3. Correcting an imposition

_____

_____

C. Assertiveness is Cross-Cultural Relationships

_____

Key Terms

self-disclosure (p. 150)

_____

_____

report-talk (p. 154)

_____

rapport-talk (p. 154)

_____

withholding feelings (p. 154)

_____

displaying feelings (p. 155)

_____

describing feelings (p. 155)

_____

describing behavior (p. 161)

_____

_____

praise (p. 161)

_____

_____

constructive criticism (p. 163)

_____

_____

assertiveness (p. 164)

_____

_____

passive behavior (p. 164)

_____

_____

aggressive behavior (p. 164)

_____

_____

Exercises

Skill Learning Activity 7.1 Test Your Competence - Building Your Vocabulary of
Emotions (p. 158)
For each statement below, select three words from the Vocabulary of Emotions listed
below that might fit the statement, but would present different emotional reactions. To
compare you choices to the authors' models, complete this activity online at the
Communicate! web site. Select student resources for Ch. 7 and then select activities.

The Vocabulary of Emotions

Words Related to *Angry*

annoyed	enraged	incensed	infuriated
irate	livid	mad	outraged

Words Related to *Loving*

affectionate	amorous	aroused	caring
fervent	heavenly	passionate	tender

Words Related to *Embarrassed*

flustered	humiliated	mortified	overwhelmed
rattled	shamefaced	sheepish	uncomfortable

Words Related to *Surprised*

astonished	astounded	baffled	jolted
mystified	shocked	startled	stunned

Words Related to *Fearful*

afraid	anxious	apprehensive	frightened
nervous	scared	terrified	worried

Words Related to *Disgusted*

aghast	appalled	dismayed	horror-struck
nauseated	repulsed	revolted	sickened

Words Related to *Hurt*

abused	damaged	forsaken	hassled
mistreated	offended	pained	wounded

Words Related to *Happy*

cheerful	contented	delighted	ecstatic
elated	glad	joyous	pleased

Words Related to *Lonely*

abandoned	alone	deserted	desolate
forlorn	isolated	lonesome	lost

Words Related to *Sad*

blue	depressed	downcast	gloomy
low	miserable	morose	sorrowful

Words Related to *Energetic*

animated	bouncy	brisk	lively
peppy	spirited	sprightly	vigorous

1. I feel _____ when you call me late at night.

2. I as _____ that she told everyone about that.

3. He was _____ when he discovered what she had done.

4. Witnessing that accident really made me feel _____.

5. when my father died I felt _____.

6. I'm _____ about graduating.

7. I'm _____ about losing my job.

8. I was _____ when the doctor told me I needed surgery.

9. I suppose I should understand that it was a mistake, but I feel _____.

10. When you look at me like that, I feel _____.

Look at each word in The Vocabulary of Emotions, say "I feel . . . ," and try to identify the feeling this word describes. Next make a list of those feelings that you recognize as ones that you experience. Then recall recent situations where you could have used each of these words. Write the message that would have been appropriate for each situation.

Skill Learning Activity 7.2 Test Your Competence – Identifying Descriptions of Feelings (p. 160)

For each statement below, determine if the message is a description of feelings. If it is, place a "D" next to it. If you determine the message is not a description of feelings, then supply a message that would be a description of feelings. You can also complete this activity online at the Communicate! web site and then compare your responses to the models provided by the authors.

1. That was a great movie!

2. I was really cheered by the flowers.

3. I feel that you not respecting my rights.

4. Yuck!

5. Damn—I screwed that up again. I feel like an idiot.

6. I feel certain I got the job because I was the most qualified person.

7. Congratulations, I feel happy for you.

8. When Pam's around, I feel like a third wheel.

9. I'm ecstatic about winning the award.

10 I'm sick and tired of you.

Skill Learning Activity 7.3 Observe and Analyze - Praising and Criticizing (p. 163)

Think of someone you need to praise and someone to whom you would like to give constructive criticism. Prepare feedback for each person in the space below. Use the following steps:
1. Begin by writing sentences that identify your general impression.
2. Recall and write down the specific behaviors, actions, and messages that led to your impression.
3. Identify all the consequences that occurred as a result.
4. If you have any advice that seems appropriate, record it.
5. Write a short feedback message that follows the guidelines for effective praise or criticism.

Skill Learning Activity 7.3 Observe and Analyze - Praising and Criticizing (p. 163), cont.

Now in the next day or two have a feedback conversation with at least one of these people and use your preparation to help you deliver the feedback. Then write a paragraph describing what happened and how well the behavior was received. Analyze why you believe the feedback was received as it was. You can also complete the preparation for this activity online at the Communicate! web site and you can email your analysis to your instructor.

Skill Learning Activity 7.4 Observe and Analyze - Passive and Aggressive Behavior (p. 166)

Describe two incidents in the past where you behaved passively or aggressively. Now analyze each situation. What type of situation was it? Did someone make a request? Did you need to express a preference or right? Was someone imposing on you? What type of relationship did you have with the person (stranger, acquaintance, friendship, business, intimate, romantic)? How did you feel about how you behaved? If you had used assertive messages what might you have said? You can also complete the preparation for this activity online at the Communicate! web site and you can email your analysis to your instructor.

<u>Skill Learning Activity 7.5 Test Your Competence – Assertive Messages (p. 168)</u>
For each of these situations, write an assertive response.

1. You come back to your dorm, apartment, or house to finish a paper that is due tomorrow, only to find that someone else is using your computer.
Assertive response:

2. You work part-time at a clothing store. Just as your shift is ending, your manager says to you, "I'd like you to work overtime, if you would. Martin's supposed to replace you, but he just called and can't get here for at least an hour." You have dinner guests arriving in two hours.
Assertive response:

3. During a phone call with your elderly grandmother, she announces, "your Great Aunt Margie called, and I told her you'd be happy to take us grocery shopping and out to lunch on Saturday. You were planning to spend Saturday working on your portfolio to take to interview next week.
Assertive response:

4, You and your friend made a date to go dancing, an activity you really enjoy. When you meet, your friend says, "If it's all the same to you, I thought we'd go to a movie instead."
Assertive response:

5. You're riding in a car with a group of friends on the way to a party when the driver begins to clown around by swerving the car back and forth, speeding up to tailgate the car in front, and honking his horn. You perceive that this driving is dangerous and you're becoming scared.
Assertive response:

Skill Learning Activity 7.6 Conversation and Analysis (p. 169)

Use your Communicate! CD-ROM to access the video clip of Trevor and Meg's conversation. Click on the "In Action" icon in the menu, then click on "Conversation Menu" in the menu bar. Select "Trevor and Meg Overview" to watch the video. As you watch Trevor and Meg discuss the future of their relationship, focus on how effectively they are communicating. How do Trevor and Meg disclose their feelings? Note how effective each is at owning feelings and opinions. How well do Trevor and Meg use praise and constructive criticism? Notice how each demonstrates the characteristics of assertive behavior. What really is Meg's fear? You can respond to these analysis questions by clicking on "Analysis" in the menu bar. When you've answered all questions, click "Done" to compare your answers to those provided by the authors.

A transcript of the conversation is printed below in a two-column format which will allow you to take notes as you watch the video.

Note: Trevor and Meg have been going together for the last several months of their senior year at college. Now that graduation is approaching, they are trying to figure out what to do about their relationship. They sit and talk.

Conversation	Analysis
Trevor: Meg, I think it's time we talk about making plans for the future. After all, we'll be graduating next month.	
Meg: Trevor, you know how uncomfortable I feel about making any long-range plans at this time. We still need to know a lot more about each other before we even think about getting engaged.	
Trevor: Why? We've both said we love each other, haven't we?	
Meg nods.	
Trevor: So why, why's this too soon? What else do we need to know?	
Meg: For starters, I'll be going to law school this fall, and this year is going to be difficult. And, you haven't gotten a job yet.	
Trevor: Come on, Meg. You're going to law	

school in the city, so I'll have a degree in business, so I can probably get a job most anywhere.

Meg: But Trevor, that's just my point. I know I'll be starting law school; I've always wanted to be a lawyer. And you don't really have any idea what you want to do. And that bothers me. I can't be worrying about you and your career when I'm going to need to focus on my classes.

Trevor: But I told you, I can get a job anywhere.

Meg: Yes, Trevor, but you need more than a job. You need to figure out what kind of job really turns you on. Or else, you risk waking up one day and regretting your life. And, I don't want to be there when that happens. I watched my dad go through a midlife crisis, and he ended up walking out on us.

Trevor: I'm not your dad, Meg. I won't leave you. And don't worry about me, I'll find a job.

Meg: Really? You know I was going to law school in the city for over a month, but you till haven't even begun a job search. Trevor, right now is the time when people are hiring and you haven't even done your resume. The longer you wait, the more difficult your search is going to be.

Trevor: Come on Meg, you've already said I'm irresistible. What company wouldn't want me?

Meg: I'm serious, Trevor. Look, I've got a scholarship to my law school, but it's only going to pay half of my expenses. I'll be taking a loan to get enough money to pay the rest and to have money to live on. I won't have the money or the time to be very supportive of you if you haven't found work. I need the security of knowing that you've got a job and that you are saving money.

Trevor: Well, they say that "two can live as cheaply as one." I was thinking that once you got settled, I'd move in and that will save us a lot of money.

Meg: Whoa, Trevor. You know how I feel about that. I do love you, and I hope that we have a future together. But living together this year is not an option. I think we need at least a year of living on our own to get ourselves settled and make sure that we really are compatible. After all, we come from totally different backgrounds. I practically raised myself, and I've paid my own bills since I was 18, while you've been lucky enough to have parents who footed your bills. There have been several times when we've talked about important issues and the differences between us have been obvious, and they worry me.

Trevor: You mean when I was joking around about our different tastes in cars?

Meg: No, Trevor, not cars, that's minor. But we also have greatly different feelings about money and family. You've told me that once you get married you want to start a family immediately. As I see it, I've got a three-year commitment to law school, then seven to ten years of hard work in order to make partner at a good firm. So I'm not sure when I want to start a family. But I know it won't be at least for six years.

Trevor: So, what are you saying, Meg? Is it over? "Thanks for the good time, Trevor, but you're not in my plans?"

Meg: Please don't be sarcastic. I'm not trying to hurt you. It makes me happy to think that we'll spend the rest of our lives together. But I'm worried about several things, so I'm just not ready to commit to that now. Let's just take a year, get settled, and see what happens. I'll love it if you do get a job near where I'm in school. That way we can have time to sort through some of the issues between us.

Trevor: You mean if you can fit me into your schedule? Meg, if we love each other now, aren't we still going to love each other next year? If we wait until we have everything settled we might never get married; there'll always be something. After all, we are two different people. We're never going to agree on everything!

Meg: Are you saying that with as unsettled that our lives are right now that we can shoulder the additional stress of planning for a marriage?

Trevor: No, what I'm saying is that we live together this year, see how it goes, then if it isn't working we don't have to get married.

_____

_____

_____

_____

_____

_____

_____

_____

_____

_____

_____

Activity 7.7 Using InfoTrac College Edition (p. 175)
As we have seen, assertiveness is sometimes perceived as aggressiveness. Using the InfoTrac College Edition subject guide, enter the term "Assertiveness." Find the article "An assertiveness training program for indecisive students attending an Italian University" *Career Development Quarterly*, June 2003 v51 i4 p322(13). Summarize the study's discussion of the relationship between assertiveness and various social skills. Were you surprised by the articles' conclusions?

Activity 7.8 Using InfoTrac College Edition
Are males really more aggressive than females on average? Are there cultural differences in what constitutes assertive behavior? Using InfoTrac College Edition, try to determine what the research suggests. Using the subject guide, enter "assertive" and locate references that focus on differences across cultures and/or genders. What did you find? Summarize your results below.

Activity 7.9 Using Technology

Sign on to an online chat room. Spend at least five minutes just "lurking" (listening). Then begin to participate in the chat. Considering both your comments and those with whom you are "chatting," how do the levels of self-disclosure differ from in-person conversations? Is there really much self-disclosure occurring? If so, how doe sit compare to self-disclosure in face-to-face encounters? How can you tell if the disclosures are truthful? Use the space below to record your observations.

(If you need an introduction to chat rooms and how to get started, enter Yahoo! Chatrooms, click on "search," and then click on "People connection chat." http://chat.yahoo.com/)

Chat room entered: _____

Activity 7.10 What would you do? A Question of Ethics (p. 169)
Read the *What Would You Do: A Question of Ethics* scenario on page 169 of your text.
Answer the following questions in the space provided here.

1. What are the ethical issues in this case?

2. Did Maria behave ethically in this situation?

3. If you were one of the women advising Maria, what would you recommend that she do?

Web Resource 7.1: Self-Disclosure and Shyness (p. 151)
For some good advice for those who are extremely reluctant to disclose, read "The Art of Self-Exposure" by Martha Beck, available through InfoTrac College Edition. Use your Communicate! CD-ROM to access Web Resource 7.1: Self-Disclosure and Shyness.

Web Resource 7.2: Becoming Vulnerable (p. 158)
To further explore how to increase your ability to be vulnerable, Use your Communicate! CD-ROM to access Web Resource 7.2: Becoming Vulnerable.

Web Resource 7.3: Gender Differences in Emotions (p. 159)
To learn about how men and women handle feelings, read the article "Gender Differences in Motives fore Regulating Emotions," available through InfoTrac College Edition. Use your Communicate! CD-ROM to access Web Resource 7.3: Gender Differences in Emotions.

Web Resource 7.4: Too Much Praise? (p. 162)
Check out an interesting article about praise and self-esteem in children, "Do You Praise Your Child Too Much?," by Ann E. LaForge, available through InfoTrac College Edition. Use your Communicate! CD-ROM to access Web Resource 7.4: Too Much Praise?

Web Resource 7.5: How to Say No (p. 166)
To learn more about refusing requests, use your Communicate! CD-ROM to access Web Resource 7.5: How to Say No.

Chapter 7 Self Test (answers and page references in Appendix)

True/False

1. Assertive behavior and aggressive behavior are the same.

2. Passive behavior is best for maintaining and improving interpersonal relationships.

3. You should always try to increase the level of self-disclosure in interpersonal relationships even if the other person does not.

4. It is best to ask permission before providing constructive criticism.

5. Early in relationships, it is best to self-disclose the kind of information you would want others to self-disclose to you.

6. Gudykunst and Kim discovered that, across cultures, self-disclosure increases as relationships become more intimate.

7. Withholding feelings is not appropriate in any situation.

Multiple Choice

1. Margie tells Estelle that she dated Tommy for a while, but she stopped when she decided his only interest in her seemed to be sexual. Margie's statement could be classified as:
    a. description of feelings
    b. self-disclosure
    c. expression of feelings
    d. passive behavior
    e. aggressive behavior

2. When in the earlier stages of a relationship, it probably is a good idea to:
    a. not self-disclose any information during your first meeting
    b. disclose information only if asked to by the other person
    c. reveal the kind of information about yourself that you want the other person to disclose to you.
    d. only disclose feelings

3. You are reviewing another student's paper. The best way to open your criticism would be:
    a. Your first paragraph is great, but some of the other paragraphs are disorganized
    b. The paper is disorganized
    c. There are many problems here, but I think we can fix them.
    d. It's ok, but…
    e. None of the above are acceptable starts to constructive criticism

4. Henry is looking over his exam. He finds a mistake in his professor's addition of his total score. If Henry behaves assertively, which of the following does he say to his professor?
    a. You made a mistake. I get 5 more points.
    b. Would you go over my test again?
    c. I'm really angry that you counted my points wrong!

d. When I counted my point total, it came to 89, five more than the total on the exam cover. Am I correct?

5. You know that someone made a mistake that impacts you, but you say nothing. This is illustrative of:
   a. assertive behavior
   b. aggressive behavior
   c. passive behavior
   d. precision
   e. none of the above

6. One of the reasons why we many people don't disclose feelings on a regular basis is:
   a. We mistake describing feelings for evaluating others
   b. We often don't have the vocabulary needed to label a range of emotions.
   c. Describing feelings is risky.
   d. All of the above are reasons why we don't disclose feelings

7. While passing by, Paul notices Anna's test grade and why she got one of her answers wrong. He then says to Anna "Hey, I see where you made a mistake on number 3 here, let me show you how to fix it." Anna reacts negatively by saying "Get away from me! Who asked for your opinion?!" Where did Paul go wrong in his attempt to offer constructive criticism to Anna:
   a. He failed to be specific
   b. He failed to ask Anna's permission before criticizing her
   c. He did not describe her feelings
   d. He failed to attend to negative face needs

8. Withholding or hiding feelings may be appropriate when
   a. you are being assertive
   b. when you are being aggressive
   c. when the situation is of little importance
   d. withholding feelings is never appropriate

Essay

1. Discuss the differences between assertive, passive and aggressive behaviors.

2. Describe the several guidelines for offering constructive criticism and why they are important.

3. What is the role of self-disclosure in the development of relationships?

4. Why can self-disclosure be risky?

5. Describe several of the reasons why many people are not good at describing feelings.

Helpful Links

http://www.mhnet.org/psyhelp/chap13/chap13i.htm **- Self-Disclosure and Openness**
Psychological Self Help by Clayton E. Tucker-Ladd offers a tutorial on how to overcome the fear of self-disclosure many people have.

http://www.mhnet.org/psyhelp/chap13/chap13j.htm **- Self-Disclosure and Openness**
This site continues the discussion found in the first site above.

http://www.minoritycareernet.com/newsltrs/96q2give.html **- Giving Constructive Criticism**
A concise list of hints for giving constructive criticism from Minority Career Network.

http://www.uiowa.edu/~ucs/asertcom.html **- Assertive Communication**
A good list of techniques on how to be assertive along with a discussion of the importance of assertiveness. This site was developed by the University of Iowa's University Counseling Service.

http://www.amanet.org/arc_center/archive/quiz_may2002.htm **- Self-Test: Assertiveness**
The American Management Association's assertiveness quiz helps to determine your level of assertiveness and then offer techniques to become more assertive.

http://www.testcafe.com/sert/ **- The Test Cafe**
Another assertiveness test. This one is from the Test Café, a website full of interesting self-quizzes.

(See your Communicate! CD-ROM for links to other websites referenced in your text.)

CHAPTER 8: Communicating in Relationships

Learning Objectives

After studying this chapter, you should be able to answer the following questions:

- What are the major types of relationships?
- What are effective ways of starting a relationship?
- How are the skills of descriptiveness, openness, tentativeness, and equality used in maintaining relationships?
- What are interpersonally effective methods of ending a relationship?
- How are electronically mediated relationships built?
- What are the five conflict styles, and when is each style appropriate?
- What skills are used to initiate conflict effectively?
- What skills are used in responding to a conflict initiated by another?

Interactive Chapter Outline

I. Types of Relationships

_____

_____

   A. Acquaintances

_____

_____

   B. Friends

_____

_____

      1. _____

      2. _____

   C. Close Friendships or Intimates

_____

_____

D. Disclosure and Feedback Ratios in Relationships

_____

_____

II. Communication in the Stages of Relationships

_____

_____

A. Beginning and Developing Relationships

_____

_____

1. _____

2. _____

3._____

B. Creating a Positive Climate in Stable Relationships

_____

_____

    1. _____

    2. _____

    3. _____

    4. _____

D. Relationship Disintegration

_____

_____

III. Electronically Mediated Relationships

    1. _____

    2. _____

    3. _____

A. From Internet to In-Person Relationships

_____

_____

B. The Dark Side of Electronically Mediated Relationships

_____

_____

_____

IV. Conflict

_____

_____

_____

   A. Styles of Managing Conflict

_____

_____

      1. Withdrawal

_____

_____

      2. Accommodating

_____

_____

      3. Forcing

_____

_____

      4. Compromising

_____

_____

      5. Collaborating

_____

_____

VI. Resolving Conflicts through Collaboration

A. Skills for Initiating Conflict

_____

_____

    1. _____

    2. _____

    3. _____

    4. _____

    5. _____

B. Responding to Conflict Effectively

_____

_____

    1. _____

    2. _____

    3. _____

    4. _____

    5. _____

C. Learning from Conflict-Management Failures

_____

_____

Key Terms

relationship (p. 176)

_____

_____

good relationship (p. 176)

_____

_____

acquaintances (p. 176)

_____

_____

friends (p. 176)

_____

_____

trust (p, 177)

_____

_____

close friends or intimates (p. 177)

_____

_____

passive (p. 180)

_____

_____

active (p. 180)

_____

_____

interactive (p. 180)

_____

_____

idea-exchange messages (p. 181)

_____

_____

gossip (p. 181)

_____

_____

stabilization (p. 182)

_____

_____

defensiveness (p. 182)

_____

_____

speaking descriptively (p. 183)

_____

_____

speaking openly (p. 183)

_____

_____

speaking tentatively (p. 183)

_____

_____

speaking as equals (p. 183)

_____

technological addiction (p. 188)

interpersonal conflict (p. 188)

withdrawal (p. 189)

mulling (p. 189)

accommodating (p. 190)

forcing (p. 191)

compromising (p. 192)

collaborating (p. 192)

Exercises

Skill Learning Activity 8.1 Observe and Analyze: Johari Window (p. 180)
Access and print out Web Resource 8.2: Johari Window Self Test at the
Communicate! web site. Take and score the "Communication Style Indicator" self-
assessment instrument. Then read the typical profiles that best fit your results.
When you have finished, write a paragraph discussing what you have learned. Did
your profile "match" what you perceive your style to be? How does this information
explain your experiences in developing and sustaining relationships? Does this
suggest any changes you need to make in order to improve your relationships?

Skill Learning Activity 8.2 Observe and Analyze: Distinguishing Between Types of
Relationships (p. 182)
1. List five people who you have known for some time who you consider to be
acquaintances. Why do you consider these people to be acquaintances rather than
friends? What do you talk about with each of these people? What subjects do you
avoid? Do any of these relationships have the potential to become friendships, if so,
what would you have to do to make that transition?

2. List five people who you have known for some time who you consider to be friends.
Why do you consider each of these people to be a friend? How does your relationship
with each differ from you relationships with your acquaintances? What do you talk about
with each of these people? What subjects do you avoid? Do any of these relationships
have the potential to become best friendships or intimate relationships? If so, what
would you have to do to make the transition?
3. List one to three people who you have known for some time who you consider to be
your best friends or your intimates. Why do you consider each of these people to be
best friends or intimates? What do you talk about with each of these people? What
subjects do you avoid? How does each of these relationships differ from those you
have with your friends?
Write an essay in which you describe what you have learned about your relationships.
You may write this essay and e-mail it to your instructor on line at the Communicate!
web site.

Skill Learning Activity 8.3 Test Your Competence: Creating Stabilizing Statements (p.
184)
Rephrase each of the messages below so that the new message fosters a supportive
rather than defensive communication climate.

1. Don't do it that way. That will never work.

2. Quit bugging me. I'll do it when I'm good and ready.

3. As long as you live in my house you'll do as I say.

4. I'll pay the bills, after all, I'm an accounting major and you're just an art major.

5. Have you decided where we're going for dinner yet?

6. You should cancel your plans. It's going to rain tomorrow.

7. I can't believe you got a tattoo. It's such a juvenile act of rebellion. You'll be sorry.

8. So, are you dating anyone?

9. Everyone drinks in college.

10. So, when do you think you'll finish that book I lent you?

Skill Learning Activity 8.4 Observe and Analyze: Advice on Cyber Relating (p. 188)

Imagine that a good friend of yours has become involved in a "serious" cyber-relationship and has asked for your advice. Based on what you have learned in this course, and your own knowledge of cyber relationships, write this friend a letter in which you give your friend educated advice on how to manage this relationship. You'll want to discuss the advantages and disadvantages of cyber relationships, but also be sure to recommend and explain specific communication skills that you have learned that might help this friend to be more effective in the relationship.

Skill Learning Activity 8.5 Observe and Analyze: Your Conflict Profile (p. 192)
Access and print out Web Resources 8.6: Your Conflict Profile", an Infotrac College
Edition article called "How do you manage conflict?" by Dawn M. Baskerville. Fill out
and score the self-assessment questionnaire and graph your results. Read the
description of each pattern. Study these results. Do they seem to capture your
perception of your conflict profile accurately? Which are your dominant styles? Are
your scores close together or are there one or two styles that seem to dominate and
other styles you prefer not to use? How does this pattern equip you to handle the
conflicts you have experienced? Based on the information from this self-assessment,
what do you need to do to become better able to handle conflict in your relationships?

Skill Learning Activity 8.6 Test Your Competence: Using the B-C-F Sequence (p. 196)
Rephrase each of these conflict messages into a statement that uses the b-c-f
sequence of describing behavior, consequences, and feelings.

1. I'm sick and tired of picking up after you. I'm not your maid. I can't go on living in a
   mess. So either clean up or get out!

2. I'm not going to sit here and let you trash my best friend. Who do you think you are
   anyway?

3. It figures you would say something like that, you're just a racist.

4. I can't believe you asked someone over for dinner at the last minute without
   asking me. That's so inconsiderate!

5. You ran up the charge card bill this month. Do you think we're made of money? If you don't stop spending we're going to go bankrupt!

Skill Learning Activity 8.7 Observe and Analyze: Correcting Conflict Failures (p. 198)

Describe a recent conflict you experienced in which the conflict was not successfully resolved. For as much as you can remember, record the "script." (Your needs or those of your partner's were unmet, or the relationship was damaged.) Analyze what happened using the concepts you have just studied. What conflict style did each of you use? Now, imagine that you could redo the conversation and you used the guidelines for collaboration. Write a script that reflects what might have happened had you been collaborative. Would this outcome have been more satisfactory? Answer the following questions. What type of conflict was this? What style did you adopt? What was the other person's style? How did styles contribute to what happened? How well did your behavior match the guidelines recommended for initiating and responding to conflict? How might o change what you did if you could "redo" this conflict episode?

Skill Learning Activity 8.8 Conversation and Analysis: Jan and Ken (p. 200)

Use your Communicate! CD-ROM to access the video clip of Jan and Ken's conversation. As you watch Jan and Ken talk, focus on how the nature of their relationship influences their interaction.

1. What does each person do to help maintain the relationship?
2. How does each person handle this conflict?
3. How well does each person listen to the other?
4. Are Jan and Ken appropriately assertive?
5. Notice how well each provides feedback and describes feelings.

You can respond to these analysis questions and compare your answers to those provided by the authors. A transcript of the conversation is printed here, which allows you to take notes as you watch the video.

Note: Jan and Ken are in their early to middle twenties. They meet at Jan's apartment. Jan and Ken have been good friends for most of their lives. But because of what she said last week, Ken believes Jan has betrayed their friendship.

Conversation

Ken: Jan, we need to talk. Why'd you tell Shannon about what happened between Katie and me? Now Shannon doesn't want to talk to me.

Jan:(*silence for a moment as she realizes he knows*) Ken, I'm sorry, I didn't mean to tell her. It just kind of slipped out when we were talking.

Ken: Sorry? Sorry is not enough. I told you that in private and you promised that you'd keep it just between you and me.

Jan: Ken, I told her that long before the two of you started dating. You know, Shannon and I, we've been friends for a long time. We were just talking about guys and cheating and stuff. It wasn't about you specifically.

Ken: It wasn't about me? It was totally about me. You had no right to tell anyone that, under any circumstances. Now Shannon doesn't trust me. She thinks I'm a lowlife that sleeps around.

Jan: Well, I'm sorry, but the two of you weren't even dating yet.

Ken: Oh, that's irrelevant. You know, it would be irrelevant even if Shannon and I weren't dating. But you know, the point is I thought I could trust you and tell you anything and that it would go no further.

Jan: Yeah, like the time I told you I was thinking about dropping out of school for a semester and you just happened to tell my dad?

Ken: Ah, that's not the same thing.

Jan: You know what, it's *exactly* the same. I trusted you and you squealed. My dad lit into

Analysis

me big-time. He should have never known I was thinking about that. I trusted you, and you betrayed me?

Ken: Well look, I was just trying to look out for you. I knew you were making a big mistake and I was just trying to stop you. And besides, you know I was right! (*gets discouraged*) Don't change the subject, here. Are you saying that you telling Shannon is some sort of payback for me telling your dad?

Jan: No, I'm just trying to point out that you've got no right to throw stones!

Ken: You know what? Then maybe neither of us can trust the other. Maybe we just shouldn't tell each other anything that we don't want broadcast to the world, huh?

Jan: Don't be such a jerk. I'm sorry, okay?

Ken: Well, that's not good enough. You ruined any chance I had with her.

Jan: Are you saying that something I said about what you did a long time ago is ruining your chances?

Ken: Yeah, it might.

Jan: Ken, if she truly valued your friendship, something that you did a long time ago shouldn't matter.

Ken: Well, maybe you're right.

Jan: Look, I said I'm sorry and I meant it. I'm also sorry about, you know, throwing in what you told my dad. I know that wasn't fair, but you know, you really hurt my feelings when you blew up at me like that.

Ken: Listen, listen, I shouldn't have, I

shouldn't have told your dad. I should have probably encouraged you to talk to him. We still friends?

_____

Activity 8.9 Using InfoTrac College Edition

How do college students deal with conflict? Using the InfoTrac College Edition subject guide, enter the term "interpersonal conflict." Find the article "Strategies to prevent and reduce conflict in college classrooms" by Steven A. Meyers. (*College Teaching*, Summer 2003 v51 i3 p94(5)) Summarize the findings here. Then click on "Interpersonal Conflict Prevention" and review some of the additional references provided. Do your findings agree with what you have read in the text?

Activity 8.10 Using InfoTrac College Edition

How does online education impact the relationship between students and teachers? Many students and teachers feel the relationship developed in a classroom setting is very important to educational success. So what happens when that face-to-face relationship is replaced with an online one? Using the InfoTrac College Edition subject guide, enter the term "online relationship." See Joan E. Thiele, Carol Allen and Mary Stucky's article "Effects of web-based instruction on learning behaviors of undergraduate and graduate students" in *Nursing and Health Care Perspectives*. Summarize the article in the space provided below. What did the authors find? Are you surprised? Why?

Activity 8.11 Using the Web

Select one of the web sites noted at the end of this chapter. Each one is indicative of the hundreds of web sites dealing with the material from this chapter. Review the site and summarize the content in the space below. Compare this material to that found in your text. What are the similarities and/or differences between the web page and the text material? Attempt to explain any differences you might find.

Activity 8.12 What Would You Do? A Question of Ethics (p. 198)

Read the *What Would You Do: A Question of Ethics* scenario on page 212 of your text. Answer the following questions in the space provided here.

1. Sort out the ethical issues in this case. Under which ethical guidelines would Sally's, Ed's, and Jamie's actions be considered ethical or unethical?

2. Using guidelines from Chapter Eight in the text, role-play different key moments in this scenario, changing them to improve the communication ethics and outcome of the situation.

Web Resource 8.1: Stages in Healthy Romantic Relationships (p. 178)
To read an interesting article about the stages of romantic relationships, use your Communicate! CD-ROM to access Web Resource 8.1: Stages in Healthy Romantic Relationships.

Web Resource 8.2: Johari Window Self-Test (p. 180)
To take and score the self-test, use your Communicate! CD-ROM to access Web Resource 8.2: Johari Window Self-Test.

Web Resource 8.3: Networking (p. 181)
To learn techniques to begin conversations in large gatherings, use your Communicate! CD-ROM to access Web Resource 8.3: Networking.

Web Resource 8.4: In-person versus Cyberspace Relationships (p. 186)
To read a thorough comparison of the differences between relationships in person and electronically mediated relationships, use your Communicate! CD-ROM to access Web Resource 8.4: In-person versus Cyberspace Relationships.

Web Resource 8.5: Bad Boys of Cyberspace (p. 188)
To read a fascinating article on deviant behavior in cyberspace, use your Communicate! CD-ROM to access Web Resource 8.5: Bad Boys of Cyberspace.

Web Resource 8.6: Your Conflict Profile (p. 192)
To fill out and score the self-assessment questionnaire, use your Communicate! CD-ROM to access Web Resource 8.6: Your Conflict Profile.

Chapter 8 Self Test (answers and page references in Appendix)

True/False

1. Avoiding conflict and preventing conflict are the same thing.

2. Each of the five styles of conflict may be appropriate in some situations.

3. There are three primary types of relationships: acquaintances, friends, and family.

4. The Johari window is a tool used to examine the relationship between disclosure and conflict.

5. There is no room for speaking tentatively when attempting to create a positive climate.

6. Stabilization is a positive communication climate that encourages satisfying conversations free of defensiveness.

7. Speaking as equals means suggesting the inaccuracy and legitimate alternative views.

Multiple Choice

1. When you risk putting your well being in the hands of another, you are showing
    a. commitment
    b. trust
    c. self-disclosure
    d. idea-exchange behaviors
    e. none of the above

2. Which of the following is not something we expect from our friends?
    a. positiveness
    b. assurance
    c. openness
    d. defensiveness

3. Kenneth and Carol are discussing their opinions on the various presidential candidates. This type of conversation contains:
    a. gossip
    b. idea-exchange messages

    c. defensiveness
    d. all of the above

4. In the middle of a conflict situation, you say "All right, you win – I don't want to fight anymore!" This is an example of
    a. withdrawal
    b. forcing
    c. bonding
    d. accommodating

5. The seductiveness of communicating electronically can result in the disruption of ongoing interpersonal relationships. This problem is often due to
    a. dishonesty
    b. technological addiction
    c. anonymity abuse
    d. accommodating

6. Thinking about or stewing over an actual or perceived problem until the conflict is perceived as being more severe and results in blaming behavior is called:
    a. mulling
    b. withdrawing
    c. stabilizing
    d. fermenting
    e. asserting

7. Angie wants to eat Italian food and see a movie. Sal wants to eat Chinese food and go to a club. Sal suggests they eat at a Chinese food restaurant, but then they go to see the movie Angie wants to see. This approach to conflict resolution
    a. is called accommodation
    b. results in both parties losing some of what they wanted
    c. may work in some situations where there is no easy answer
    d. all of the above

8. It is a good idea to mentally rehearse what you will say in a conflict situation before you confront the other person because
    a. we need to be defensive
    b. we need to be seen as having a strong argument
    c. we need to be in control of our emotions
    d. we need to have an extended argument

Essay

1. Discuss the five styles of conflict. What are they and when are they appropriate?

2. What are the different strategies that you can use to get information about another? Why is this important for developing relationships?

3. Summarize the skills used to effectively initiate conflict.

4. Summarize the skills used to effectively respond to a conflict initiated by another.

5. What is the JoHari window and what is it used to explain? Can the shape of the "panes" change? Why?

Helpful Links

http://www3.azwestern.edu/psy/dgershaw/lol/marriages.last.htm - **Why Marriages Last**
This site by David Gershaw examines seven reasons why partners think their marriages last.
http://www.etsu.edu/philos/faculty/hugh/honesty.htm - **Honesty and Intimacy**
An article from *Journal of Social and Personal Relationships* explores the role of honesty in developing and maintaining personal relationships. By G. Graham and H. LaFollette.
http://humanresources.about.com/careers/humanresources/cs/conflictresolves/index.htm?iam=dpile&terms=%2Binterpersonal+%2Bconflict – **Conflict Resolution/Controversy Management**
A long address, but one that leads to a useful site that explores conflict resolution and management.
http://pertinent.com/pertinfo/business/kareCom3.html - **Six Ways to Get Along Better**
This site by Kare Anderson looks at simple strategies for preventing conflicts.
http://www.geocities.com/research93/ - **Close Relationships and Personality**

Research Web Site
Close Relationships and Personality Research Web Site has a fun and interesting personality quiz that helps determine your "attachment style."

(See your Communicate! CD-ROM for links to other websites referenced in your text.)

CHAPTER 9: Interviewing

Learning Objectives

After studying this chapter, you should be able to answer the following questions:

- What is an interview?
- What types of questions are used in an interview?
- What are the characteristics of open and closed, primary and secondary, and neutral and leading questions?
- How do you prepare for and conduct an information interview?
- How do you conduct a job interview?
- How should you prepare a resume and cover letter so that you are likely to be chosen for a job interview?
- How should you prepare to be interviewed?
- Can you identify typical questions used by job interviewers?
- What can you do to follow up an interview?

Interactive Chapter Outline

I. Questions Used in Interviewing

_____

_____

    A. Open versus closed Questions

        1. _____

        _____

        2. _____

        _____

    B. Neutral versus Leading Questions

        1. _____

_____

    2. _____

    _____

C. Primary versus Secondary Questions

    1. _____

    _____

    2. _____

    _____

II. Interviewing for Information

_____

_____

A. Define the Purpose of the Interview

_____

_____

B. Select the Best Person to Interview

_____

_____

C. Developing the Interview Protocol

_____

_____

D. Conducting the Interview

_____

_____

III. Conducting Employment Interviews

_____

_____

A. Preparing for the Interview

_____

_____

B. Conducting the Interview

_____

_____

IV. Interviewing to Get a Job

_____

_____

A. Getting the Interview

_____

_____

1. It all begins with research

_____

_____

2. Write an effective cover letter

_____

_____

3. Prepare a professional resume

_____

_____

4. Electronic cover letters and resumes

_____

_____

B. Preparing to be Interviewed

_____

_____

1.

_____

_____

2.

_____

_____

3.

_____

4. _____

_____

_____

5. _____

_____

_____

6. _____

_____

_____

C. Behavior During the Interview

_____

_____

1. _____

_____

_____

2. _____

_____

_____

3. _____

_____

_____

4.

_____

_____

5.

_____

_____

D. Interview Follow-Up

_____

_____

Key Terms

interview (p. 206)

_____

_____

open questions (p. 206)

_____

_____

closed questions (p. 206)

_____

_____

neutral questions (p. 207)

_____

_____

leading questions (p. 207)

_____

_____

primary questions (p. 207)

_____

_____

secondary or follow-up questions (p. 207)

_____

_____

interview protocol (p. 209)

_____

_____

cover letter (p. 214)

_____

_____

resume (p. 214)

_____

_____

electronic cover letters and resumes (p. 215)

_____

_____

Exercises

Skill Learning Activity 9.1 Test Your Competence – Open and Closed Questions (p. 208)

Indicate which of the following questions are open (O) and which are closed (C). If the question is open, write a closed question seeking similar information; if the questions is closed, write an open question. Make sure that your questions are neutral rather than leading.

____ 1. What leads you to believe that Sheldon will be appointed?

____ 2. How many steps are there in getting a book into print?

____ 3. Will you try out for the Shakespearean play this year?

____ 4. When are you getting married?

____ 5. Have you participated in the garden project?

Skill Learning Activity 9.2 Observe and Analyze – Information Interviews (p. 211)
Select a televised interview (for example, a news program, infomercial, or congressional hearing) for analysis. You may want to video tape it so you can watch it several times. Using the worksheet below, count the number of open, closed, neutral, leading, and follow-up questions. After viewing the interview, analyze it. Was there a good balance of questions? Did the interviewer as appropriate follow-up questions? What was the apparent goal of the interview? Was it reached? What grade would you give the interviewer? Why? What were the interviewer's strengths? Weaknesses? When you have finished analyzing the interview, write a paragraph discussing your analysis in the space below. The worksheet is also available at the Communicate! web site.

Questions Type Tally

Questions	Open	Closed	Total
Neutral			
Leading			
Follow-up			
Total			

Skill Learning Activity 9.3 Observe and Analyze – Interviewing an Interviewer (p. 213)

Make an appointment to interview a human resource manager who is responsible for employment interviewing. Prepare an interview protocol that probes this manager about his or her interviewing practices. After the interview, compare this manager's practice to the text discussion. Submit your protocol, interview notes, and a short essay that describes what you have learned to your instructor. You may complete this activity online and e-mail it to your instructor.

Skill Learning Activity 9.4 Test Your Competence – Resume and Cover Letter (p. 215)

Read the help wanted ads in your local newspaper until you locate a job you would enjoy. Write a résumé and cover letter applying for this position. To link you to an online resume service to draft and print your resume, use your Communicate! CD-ROM to access Web Resource 9.9: Résumé Builder. When you have completed your résumé and cover letter, if requested, submit them to your instructor.

Skill Learning Activity 9.5 Conversation and Analysis: Elliott Miller's Interview (p. 221)

Use your Communicate! CD-ROM to access the video clip of Elliott Miller's job interview at Community Savings and Loan. As you watch the video, notice how well both Karen Bourne and Elliott Miller follow the guidelines for effective interviews. You can record your observations and respond to other analytical questions by clicking on "Analysis" in the menu bar. When you've answered all the questions, click "Done" to compare your answers with those provided y the authors. A transcript of the conversation is printed below which allows you to take notes as you watch the video.

Note: Elliott Miller is a second-semester senior who has double-majored in business and communication. Today he is interviewing with Community Savings and Loan, which is recruiting managerial trainees. Elliott has dressed carefully. He has on his good charcoal suit, a light blue shirt, a conservative necktie, and wingtips. At 10am sharp he knocks on the office door of Karen Bourne, the person with whom he has an interview. She is in her mid-thirties and dressed in a conservative navy blue suit. She opens the door and offers her hand to Elliott.

Conversation	Analysis
Bourne: Mr. Miller, I see you're right on time. That's a good start. *(They shake hands.)*	_____ _____
Miller: Thank you for inviting me to interview	_____

today.

Bourne: Slt down. *(He sits in the chair in front of her desk; she sits behind the desk.)* So you're about to finish college are you? I remember that time in my own life——exciting and scary!

Miller: It's definitely both for me. I'm particularly excited about the job here at Community Savings and Loan.

Bourne: *(smiles)* Then there's a mutual interest. We had a lot of applications, but we're interviewing only eight of them. What I'd like to do is get a sense of your interests and tell you about our managerial trainee program here, so that we can see if the fit between us is as good as it looks on paper. Sound good to you?

Miller: Great.

Bourne: Let me start by telling you about a rather common problem we've had with our past managerial trainees. Many of them run into a problem——something they have trouble learning or doing right. That's normal enough — we expect that. But a lot of trainees seem to get derailed when that happens. Instead of finding another way to approach the problem, they get discouraged and give up. So I'm very interested in hearing what you've done when you've encountered problems or road blocks in your life.

Miller: Well, I can remember one time when I hit a real road block. I was taking an advanced chemistry course, and I just couldn't seem to understand the material. I failed the first exam, even though I'd studied

failed the first exam, even though I'd studied hard.

Bourne: Good example of a problem. What did you do?

Miller: I started going to all the tutorial sessions that grad assistants offer. That helped a little but I still wasn't getting the material the way I should. So, I organized a study team and offered to pay for pizzas so that students who were on top of the class would have a reason to come.

Bourne: *(nodding with admiration)* That shows a lot of initiative and creativity. Did the study team work?

Miller: *(smiling)* It sure did. I wound up getting a B in the course, and so did several other members of the study team who had been in the same boat I was in early in the semester.

Bourne: So you don't mind asking for help if you need it?

Miller: I'd rather do that than flounder, but I'm usually pretty able to operate independently.

Bourne: So you prefer working on your own to working with others?

Miller: That depends on the situation or project. If I have all that I need to do something on my own, I'm comfortable working solo. But there are other cases in which I don't have everything I need to do something well — maybe I don't have experience in some aspect of the job or I don't have a particular skill or I don't understand some perspectives on the issues. In cases like that, I thing teams are more effective than individuals.

Bourne: Good. Banking management requires the ability to be self-initiating and also the ability to work with others. Let me ask another question. As I was looking over your transcript and resume, I noticed that you changed your major several times. Does that indicate you have difficulty making a commitment and sticking with it?

Miller: I guess you could think that, but it really shows that I was willing to explore a lot of alternatives before making a firm commitment.

Bourne: But don't you think that you wasted a lot of time and courses getting to that commitment?

Miller: I don't think so. I learned something in all of the course I took. For instance, when I was a philosophy major, I learned about logical thinking and careful reasoning. That's going to be useful to me in management. When I was majoring in English, I learned how to write well and how to read others' writing critically. That's going to serve me well in management too.

Bourne: So what led you to your final decision to double major in business and communication? That's kind of an unusual combination.

Miller: It seems a very natural one to me. I wanted to learn bout business because I

wanted to learn bout business because I
want to be a manager in an organization. I
need to know how organizations work and I
need to understand different management
philosophies and styles. At the same time,
managers work with people, and that means I
have to have strong communication skills.

_____

_____

_____

_____

_____

Skill Learning Activity 9.6 Test Your Competence: Mock Interview (p. 223)

Pair with one of your classmates and conduct mock interviews. You and your
classmate should exchange the material you prepared in Activity 9.4. You will prepare
and participate in two interviews, one in which you will use your partner's ad, resume,
and cover letter to prepare and interview your partner for a job, and the other in which
your partner will use the material you supply to interview you for a job. Your instructor
will provide you will additional information regarding this assignment.

Activity 9.7 Using InfoTrac College Edition

Under the subject "cover letter," see "Quick! Take cover! A cover letter is your best
ticket to a great job--if you know how to write a good one!," by Tamra B. Orr in *Career
World*, Jan 2003 v31 i4 p20(2). Compare the article's recommendations with those
from your text. Note at least three ideas on preparing cover letters that you would want
to follow.

Activity 9.8 Using InfoTrac College Edition
What skills are required for today's jobs? Using the subject guide, use the search term "job skills." Review several articles and summarize what they say about the importance of job skills in the employment marketplace. What skills are important? How are organizations ensuring future employees get these skills? Do you think necessary skills have changed over time? Why?

Activity 9.9 Using Technology
Many career-oriented web sites like Monster.com not only allow job seekers to browse through job listings, they also offer the ability to post your resume online so that organizations that are seeking applicants may review your qualifications online. Go to one of the career search web sites listed at the end of this chapter and complete the online registration and resume submission process. Some sites allow you to upload a file containing your resume, while others ask you to fill out an online form. Also complete the "career profile" or other online questionnaire used to establish the types of jobs you are seeking or are qualified for. Use your actual list of qualifications and skills, location preference, salary range, etc. Periodically check back to the website and note how many times your resume was viewed and if any potential employers contacted you via e-mail or phone. Be prepared to share your results with the class.

Activity 9.10 What Would You Do? A Question of Ethics (p. 224)
Read the *What Would You Do: A Question of Ethics* scenario on page 224 of your text. Answer the following questions in the space provided here.

1. Is it interpersonally ethical for Mark to follow Ken's advice? Why?

2. How should we deal with statements like "Everybody does it"?

Web Resource 9.1: Email Interviews (p. 211)
To read some useful tips for conducting electronic interviews using email, use your Communicate! CD-ROM to access Web Resource 9.1: Email interviews.

Web Resource 9.2: 109 Typical Job Interview Questions (p. 212)
For a list of potential interview questions, use your Communicate! CD-ROM to access
Web Resource 9.2: 109 Typical Job Interview Questions.

Web Resource 9.3: Discrimination Laws and Interviewing (p. 212)
To read a generalized discussion of the types of questions that should not be asked in
interviews, use your Communicate! CD-ROM to access Web Resource 9.3:
Discrimination Laws and Interviewing.

Web Resource 9.4: Research Before You Write (p. 214)
To read a generalized discussion of the types of questions that should not be asked in
interviews, use your Communicate! CD-ROM to access Web Resource 9.4: Research
Before You Write.

Web Resource 9.5: Quick Take Cover (p. 214)
To read a generalized discussion of the types of questions that should not be asked in
interviews, use your Communicate! CD-ROM to access Web Resource 9.5: Quick Take
Cover.

Web Resource 9.6: Cover Letter Don'ts (p. 214)
To read a list of several cover letter faux pas that you will want to avoid, use your
Communicate! CD-ROM to access Web Resource 9.6: Cover Letter Don'ts.

Web Resource 9.7: What is your Objective? (p. 214)
To read more about formulating career objective statements, use your Communicate!
CD-ROM to access Web Resource 9.7: What is your Objective?

Web Resource 9.8: Resume Pet Peeves (p. 215)
To read about –and avoid- the top twenty resume pet peeves identified by 2,500
recruiters, use your Communicate! CD-ROM to access Web Resource 9.8: Resume
Pet Peeves.

Web Resource 9.9: Resume Builder (p. 215)
To link to an online resume service to draft and print your resume, use your
Communicate! CD-ROM to access Web Resource 9.9: Resume Builder.

Web Resource 9.10: Monster.com's Resume Dos and Don'ts (p. 218)
For more information on electronic resumes, use your Communicate! CD-ROM to
access Web Resource 9.10: Monster.com's Resume Dos and Don'ts.

Web Resource 9.11: Virtual Interview (p. 219)
To sharpen your interview skills, answer sample questions, and receive help to improve
your answers, use your Communicate! CD-ROM to access Web Resource 9.11: Virtual
Interview.

 Web Resource 9.12: Notable Notes (p. 223)
For tips on writing thank-you notes, use your Communicate! CD-ROM to access Web
Resource 9.12: Notable Notes.

Chapter 9 Self Test (answers and page references in Appendix)

True/False

1. Despite the proliferation of electronic forms of communication, it is still not possible
to apply for jobs online or submit resumes online.

2. You should plan to arrive 10-15 minutes prior to your appointment for an interview.

3. The job interview is not a place for the job candidate to ask questions of the
interviewer.

4. Open questions are broad-based questions designed to allow the interviewee to
respond however he or she wishes.

5. Follow-up questions are planned or unplanned questions designed to further probe
the answer to a primary question.

6. Closed questions allow the interviewee the opportunity to control the interview and
take up additional time.

7. In most types of interviews, neutral questions are to be avoided.

Multiple Choice

1. Which of the following is not a good thing to do in a cover letter?
    a. include your qualifications
    b. include contact information
    c. ask for an interview only indirectly
    d. keep it short
    e. all of thc above are ok.

2. If an interviewer wants an interviewee to express details, ideas and feelings, the interviewer will most likely avoid using
    a. leading questions
    b. open questions
    c. follow-up questions
    d. closed questions

3. Which of the following behaviors is not advised by your text?
    a. starting a conversation about salary and benefits
    b. learning about the company
    c. asking about your specific duties within the company
    d. acting as if you want the job
    e. showing up early for the interview appointment

4. Electronic cover letters and resumes
    a. have become increasingly popular
    b. may be different from paper versions in several ways
    c. usually should be kept simple in format
    d. can be sifted electronically
    e. all of the above

5. References
    a. a part of the resume
    b. should include full contact information
    c. are people who will speak well of you
    d. should never be part of the resume
    e. a-c only

6. Questions an interviewee might be expected to ask in an interview include
    a. Can you describe a typical work day?
    b. What is the biggest challenge in this job?

    c. Interviewees should not ask questions during an interview

    d. a and b

7. Regarding interview follow-up:

    a. thank you notes are never read, so don't bother writing one

    b. do not contact the interviewer, you will only be seen as desperate

    c. it is acceptable to contact your interviewer for feedback even if you don't get the job.

    d. none of the above

8. Interviewing for information

    a. can be used by students conducting research

    b. is more likely to be successful if well-planned in advance

    c. requires an interview protocol

    d. can be used by health care professionals

    e. all of the above

Essay

1. Discuss the different types of interview questions and their purposes.

2. What are the key points of information that should be included in a resume?

3. Describe the differences between an electronic resume and a conventional resume. Why do these differences exist?

4. Discuss key elements involved in preparation for an interview.

5. How should one behave during an interview? Include a discussion of non-verbal elements.

Helpful Links

http://www.monster.com – **Monster.com**
A free site for posting your resume and looking for jobs. You can search by location, job type, etc.

http://www.employment911.com – **Employment 911**
similar to Monster.com, employment911 claims to have over three million job listings.

http://jobsearch.about.com/careers/jobsearch/cs/interviews/index.htm - **Job Searching**

This site from About.com offers a long list of interview resources including a long list of questions commonly asked by interviewers and a long list of questions interviewees should consider asking. Also, tips on dress, thank you notes and other topics.

http://www2.volstate.edu/humanities/comm/careers.htm - **Careers for Communication Majors**
This site offers a long list of career resources for communication majors, but it is also useful for job seekers from other fields as well. A good list of links from the Department of Communication at Volunteer State Community College.

http://www.jobweb.com/Resumes_Interviews/default.htm - **JobWeb Resumes and Interviews**
Tips for resume and cover letter writing. The main Jobweb.com site is also very useful.

(Many colleges and universities have resources available for their students and graduates to assist them in career placement. Check your school's web site for more information.) (See your Communicate! CD-ROM for links to other websites referenced in your text.)

III

GROUP COMMUNICATION

CHAPTER 10: Participating in Group Communication

Learning Objectives

After studying this chapter, you should be able to answer the following questions:
- What characterizes effective groups?
- How can group discussion lead to improving group goal statements?
- What is the optimum size for a group?
- What factors affect cohesiveness in groups?
- How can a group improve its cohesiveness?
- How do groups form, maintain, and change their norms?
- How does the physical setting affect group interaction?
- What are the stages of group development?
- What are the steps of the problem-solving method?
- What constraints result in groups being ineffective at problem-solving, and how can they be managed?

Interactive Chapter Outline

I. Characteristics of Effective Work Groups

_____

_____

   A. Clearly Defined Goals

_____

_____

   B. Optimum Number of Diverse Members

_____

_____

   C. Cohesiveness

_____

_____

D. Norms

_____

_____

E. The Working Environment

_____

_____

II. Stages of Group Development

_____

_____

A. Forming

_____

_____

B. Storming

_____

_____

C. Norming

_____

_____

D. Performing

_____

_____

E. Adjourning

_____

_____

III. Problem Solving in Groups

_____

_____

A. Defining the Problem

_____

_____

1. _____

2. _____

3. _____

4. _____

5. _____

6. _____

7. _____

B. Analyzing the Problem

_____

_____

C. Determining Solution Criteria

_____

_____

D. Identifying Possible Solutions

_____

_____

E. Evaluating Solutions

_____

_____

F. Deciding

_____

_____

1. _____

2. _____

3. _____

4. _____

5. _____

IV. Constraints on Effective Decision Making

_____

_____

1. _____

2. _____

3. _____

Key Terms

work group (p. 230)

_____

_____

group goal (p. 230)

_____

_____

specific goal (p. 230)

_____

_____

consistent goals (p. 230)

_____

_____

challenging goals (p. 231)

_____

_____

acceptable goals (p. 231)

_____

_____

homogenous group (p. 232)

heterogeneous group (p. 232)

cohesiveness (p. 232)

team building activities (p. 233)

norms (p. 234)

ground rules (p. 234)

working environment (p. 235)

forming (p. 237)

storming (p. 238)

groupthink (p. 238)

norming (p. 239)

performing (p. 239)

adjourning (p. 239)

questions of fact (p. 242)

questions of value (p. 242)

questions of policy (p. 242)

decision making (p. 246)

cognitive constraints (p. 250)

_____

_____

affiliative constraints (p. 250)

_____

_____

devil's advocate (p. 250)

_____

_____

egocentric constraints (p. 250)

_____

_____

Exercises

Skill Learning Activity 10.1 Observe and Analyze: Cohesiveness in Homogeneous Groups versus Heterogeneous Groups (p. 234)

Identify two groups (for example a sports team, study group, fraternal or community group, or work team) to which you belong, one should have members who you consider to be homogeneous the other, members who you consider to be heterogeneous. Analyze the demographic differences in each group. When you have completed this analysis, write a paragraph that discusses cohesiveness in each group. How cohesive is each group? Are both groups equally cohesive? Was it easier or more difficult to establish cohesiveness in a particular group? What real or potential pitfalls result from the level of cohesiveness in each group?

Use the demographic analysis worksheet that follows to help you with this task. Additional copies of this worksheet can be downloaded from the Communicate! Web site.

Skill Learning Activity 10.1 **Demographic Analysis Worksheet**

Name	Group	Age	Sex	Sexual orien-tation	Race	Education	Ethnicity	Social/economic class	Religion	Native language

Skill Learning Activity 10.2 Observe and Analyze: Stages of Group Development (p. 240)

Think of a group to which you have belonged for less than one quarter, semester, or term (if you have an assigned group in this course, use that group). Now, write a paragraph that begins by identifying the stage of development the group is currently in and then describes how this group transitioned through each of the previous stages of group development. What event(s) do you recall as turning points, marking the group's movement from one stage to another. Has the group become "stuck" in a stage, or has it developed smoothly? What factors contributed to that? What can you do to help this group succeed in the stage that it is in and transition to the next stage? You can choose to complete this activity online at the Communicate! web site and, if requested, email it to your instructor.

Skill Learning Activity 10.3 Test Your Competence: Stating Problems (p. 243)

Indicate whether each of the following is a question of fact (F), a question of value (V), or a question of policy (P). You can complete this activity online and compare your answers to the authors'.

_____ 1. What should we do to increase the quality of finished parts?

_____ 2. Do police stop African American drivers more frequently than other drivers?

_____ 3. Should television news organizations use exit polls to call elections?

_____ 4. Is John guilty of involuntary manslaughter?

_____ 5. Is seniority the best method of handling employee layoffs?

_____ 6. What is the best vacation plan for our family?

Skill Learning Activity 10.4 Test Your Competence: The Problem-Solving Process (p. 248)

Describe how you would use the six steps in the problem solving process to arrive at a solution to the following situation.

Your manager at work has decided that you and your co-workers should decide whether it is time to upgrade your company supplied mobile phone hardware and service. If you decided to upgrade, you are suppose to do the research and choose the equipment and service provider.

Activity 10.5: Homogenous and Heterogeneous Groups
Visit the web site of a large company, such as General Motors, General Electric, or Coca Cola. Search the site and find the names and brief background sketches of the members of the Board of Directors. Analyze the ways in which the members are similar or different. Answer the following questions in the space provided below:

1. What relevant knowledge and skills might each bring to the group's decision process?

2. What viewpoints are not represented by the board members?

3. How might an absence of these viewpoints affect their discussions?

Activity 10.6 Physical Settings
During the next week, keep a record of all the group settings you participate in. Note the physical setting (location, temperature, size of space, seating configuration), the interaction patterns (who talks, who listens, who agrees, who disagrees), and your satisfaction with the group discussion (high to low). At the end of the week, analyze these data to see how the physical settings might have influenced group interaction and your satisfaction with the process. What conclusions can you draw?

Physical Setting:

Interaction Patterns:

Satisfaction:

Analysis:

Activity 10.7 – Decision Methods
Remember an instance where a group you were part of made a poor decision using a majority-rule method. In the space provided below, analyze why the decision was a poor one. Answer the following questions: Would a different decision method have helped? If so, what method might have been more effective? Why?

Activity 10.8 Using InfoTrac College Edition
How can we improve our ability to brainstorm effectively? Under the subject "problem solving discussion," click on "periodical references." Scroll to "group problem solving." Find the article "Some Brainstorming Exercises," by Ethan M. Rasiel. (*Across the Board*, June 2000.) Summarize the article's techniques here.

10.9 Using InfoTrac College Edition
Locate the article titled "How to get a group to perform like a team," by Blanchard, Carew and Parsi-Carew. (*Training & Development*, Sept 1996 v50 n9 p34(4)) Do you think the PERFORM method would work in a classroom? Next, scroll down to Work Groups and click on the "Periodical References" button. Locate other articles that discuss similar ideas. Compare these articles to the textbook. How are they similar ?

Activity 10.10 What Would You Do?   A Question of Ethics (p. 250)
Read the *What Would You Do: A Question of Ethics* scenario on page 250 of your text. Answer the following questions in the space provided here.

1. What did the group really know about the Boardman Center? Is it good group discussion practice to rely on a passing comment on one member?

2. Regardless of whether the meeting went smoothly, is there any ethical problem with this process? Explain.

Web Resource 10.1: Setting Group Goals (p. 230)
To read about various methods that can be used to arrive at group goals, use your Communicate! CD-ROM to access Web Resource 10.1: Setting Group Goals.

Web Resource 10.2: Setting Group Norms (p. 234)
To read a list of group norms that contribute to group effectiveness, use your Communicate! CD-ROM to access Web Resource 10.2: Setting Group Norms.

Web Resource 10.3: Social Norm Interventions (p. 235)
To read about social norm theory, use your Communicate! CD-ROM to access Web Resource 10.3: Social Norm Interventions.

Web Resource 10.4: Forming Fears and Uncertainty (p. 238)
To explore the specific anxieties raised in a new group situation, use your Communicate! CD-ROM to access Web Resource 10.4: Forming Fears and Uncertainty.

Web Resource 10.5: Groupthink (p. 239)
To read a comprehensive article on groupthink, use your Communicate! CD-ROM to access Web Resource 10.5: Groupthink.

Web Resource 10.6: What's Your Problem? (p. 241)
To read about various methods that can be used to arrive at group goals, use your Communicate! CD-ROM to access Web Resource 10.6: What's Your Problem?

Web Resource 10.7: Decision-Making Methods (p. 247)
To read a complete comparison of the advantages and disadvantages of various decision-making methods, use your Communicate! CD-ROM to access Web Resource 10.8: Decision-Making Methods.

Chapter 10 Self Test (answers and page references in Appendix)

True/False

1. Effective groups are most likely to be made up of heterogeneous members.

2. The consensus method for group decision-making is the same thing as a unanimous decision.

3. The expert opinion method for deciding puts final responsibility for a decision in the hands of a person outside the group with great knowledge or expertise in the matter.

4. Physical location and setting have little impact on the workings of a group.

5. "A collection of three or more people who must interact and influence one another to accomplish a common purpose" is the definition of a work group.

6. In a group that is not cohesive, members may be indifferent towards the group goal, not like each other, and work in ways that prevent the group from being successful.

7. Effective group norms can only be developed through the adoption of formal ground rules.

Multiple Choice

1. The process of choosing among alternatives is
    a. decision making
    b. norming
    c. performing

    d. storming

2. "What should we do to reduce air pollution?" is an example of what type of question?
    a. question of fact
    b. question of policy
    c. question of value
    d. question of norming
    e. question of skill

3. Tanya shows up late for a group meeting. The discussion had already begun and as she entered the room, she was greeted by several angry looks. Which of the following best explains their reaction to Tanya's tardiness?
    a. storming was in progress
    b. norms had not yet been established
    c. groupthink was occurring
    d. an on-time norm had been developed by that group

4. Adjourning is
    a. the end of the meeting
    b. the stage of group development where members assign meaning to what they have done
    c. the stage of group development concerned with the establishment of group standards
    d. none of the above

5. A group decides to define the problem it has been tasked to decide as follows: "Should the company abolish the current pension plan and abolish the current dental plan." This group has committed which error in problem consideration:
    a. The problem should use specific and precise language.
    b. The problem should be stated as a question.
    c. The problem should be a policy issue.
    d. The problem should contain only one central idea.
    e. The group has committee no error.

6. Groupthink
    a. is to be commended, it shows the group members are all on the same page.
    b. is the result of storming
    c. can be prevented by avoiding disagreement
    d. none of the above are true in relation to groupthink

7. The group looks like it has achieved a consensus on the wording of the new campus-wide non-discrimination policy. Just then Sandy speaks up and says "I don't

think the penalties are severe enough in Section III." A discussion ensues that re-affirms the group's decision. Sandy's comment was an example of:
- a. affiliative constraint
- b. storming
- c. devil's advocate
- d. groupthink

8. Derrick gets up in the group and says "I know most of you are new to the group, but I've been here for years and know what will and won't work." This is a sure sign that the group will have to face:
- a. egocentric constraints
- b. cognitive constraints
- c. storming
- d. devil's advocate
- e. none of the above

Essay

1. Discuss the three different types of questions. How are each type identified?

2. What are the characteristics of an ideal group goal? Why are such goals important to the effective functioning of a work group?

3. Discuss the stages of group development. Label each and note why it is important.

4. What are the six key tasks a group faces when attempting to make a decision?

5. Discuss the pros and cons of each of the methods of group decision making.

Helpful Links

http://en.wikipedia.org/wiki/Groupthink - **Groupthink**
From Wikipedia, this site discusses groupthink and offers links to additional resources.

http://www.mapnp.org/library/grp_skll/theory/theory.htm - **Group Dynamics**
Assembled by Carter McNamara, this site looks at the basic nature of groups and how they develop.

http://www.montana.edu/wwwpb/pubs/mt8401.html - **Setting Group Goals**
This site, from the Montana State University Extension Service, explores the rationale for having group goals.

http://projects.edtech.sandi.net/staffdev/tpss99/processguides/brainstorming.html -
Brainstorming
From process Guides, a brief guide to how to brainstorm

http://www.jpb.com/creative/brainstorming.php - Brainstorming
Another guide to brainstorming, from Bwiti.

http://www.jpb.com/brainstormer/index.php - **Brainstorming Software**
A link to free (trial) software that is designed to improve the brainstorming process and
results. From Bwiti.

(See your Communicate! CD-ROM for links to other websites referenced in your text.)

CHAPTER 11: Members' Roles and Leadership in Groups

Learning Objectives

After studying this chapter, you should be able to answer the following questions:

- What are roles, and why are they important in groups?
- How do members choose their roles?
- What types of roles do members of groups enact?
- What behaviors are expected of all members to make group meetings effective?
- What is leadership and why is it important to a group?
- What are the tasks of leadership?
- What characterizes the communication behavior of leaders?
- How does leadership develop in a group?
- What behaviors can help an individual become a leader?
- What should the leader of a meeting do to make the meeting successful?

Interactive Chapter Outline

I. Members' Roles

_____

_____

  A. Task-oriented Roles

_____

_____

     1. _____

     2. _____

     3. _____

  B. Maintenance Roles

_____

_____

   1. _____

   2. _____

   3. _____

   4. _____

C. Procedural Roles

_____

_____

   1. _____

   2. _____

   3. _____

D. Self-Centered Roles

_____

_____

   1. _____

   2. _____

   3. _____

   4. _____

E. Normal Distribution of Roles

_____

_____

II. Member Responsibilities in Group Meetings

_____

_____

A. Preparing for the Meeting

_____

_____

1. _____

2. _____

3. _____

4. _____

5. _____

B. Participating in the Meeting

_____

_____

. _____

2. _____

3. _____

4. _____

5. _____

6. _____

C. Following-up the Meeting

_____

_____

    1. _____

    2. _____

    3. _____

    4. _____

    5. _____

    6. _____

III. Leadership

_____

_____

A. The Function of Leadership

_____

_____

B. Types of Leaders

_____

_____

    1. _____

    2. _____

C. How Members Gain and Maintain Informal Leadership

_____

_____

1. _____

2. _____

3. _____

4. _____

5. _____

D. Gender Differences in Emerging Leaders

_____

_____

IV. Leading Group Meetings

_____

_____

A. Before the Meeting

_____

_____

1. _____

2. _____

3. _____

4. _____

5. _____

B. During the Meeting

_____

_____

    1. _____

    2. _____

    3. _____

    4. _____

    5. _____

    6. _____

    7. _____

    8. _____

C. Meeting Follow-up

_____

_____

    1. _____

    2. _____

    3. _____

    4. _____

V. Evaluating Group Effectiveness

_____

A. The Decision

_____

_____

B. Individual Participation and Role Behavior

_____

_____

C. Leadership

_____

_____

Key Terms

roles (p. 256)

_____

_____

task-related roles (p. 256)

_____

_____

information or opinion givers (p. 256)

_____

_____

information or opinion seekers (p. 256)

_____

_____

analyzers (p. 256)

_____

_____

maintenance roles (p. 257)

_____

_____

supporters (p. 257)

_____

_____

tension relievers (p. 257)

_____

_____

harmonizers (p. 257)

_____

_____

interpreters (p. 257)

_____

_____

procedural roles (p. 257)

_____

_____

expediters (p. 258)

_____

_____

recorders (p. 258)

minutes (p. 258)

gatekeeper (p. 258)

self-centered roles (p. 258)

aggressors (p. 259)

jokers (p. 259)

withdrawers (p. 259)

monopolizers (p. 259)

leadership (p. 263)

formal leader (p. 264)

_____

informal leader (p. 264)

_____

framing (p. 265)

_____

Exercises

<u>Skill Learning Activity 11.1 Test Your Competence: Identifying Roles (p. 260)</u>
Match the typical comment to the role it is most characteristic of. You may use the
worksheet below or complete this activity at the Communicate! web site.

Identifying Roles Worksheet

Typical Comment	Roles
____ 1. "Did any one discover if we have to recommend only one company?"	a. aggressor
____ 2. "I don't have time to help with that."	b. analyzer
____ 3. "I think Rick has an excellent idea."	c. expediter
____ 4. "Stupid idea, Katie. Why don't you think before you open your mouth."	d. gatekeeper
____ 5. "Kwitabe doesn't necessarily agree with you, but he would consider it rude to openly disagree with someone who is older."	e. harmonizer f. information or opinion giver
____ 6. "Josiah, in your plan, weren't you assuming that we'd only need two	g. information or opinion seeker

days for rehearsal?"	h. interpreter
___ 7. "Lisa, I understand your point. What do you think about it, Paul?"	i. supporter
___ 8. "O.K., so we've all agreed that we should begin keeping time logs. Now shouldn't we be thinking about what information needs to be in them?"	j. tension reliever k. withdrawer
___ 9. " Wow, it's getting tense in here. If we don't chill out soon, we're likely to spontaneously combust. And, hello, that'll be a problem, cuz, we're the only engine company in this area of town. Right?"	
___ 10. "Barb, I don't think that your position is really that different from Saul's. Let me see if I can explain how they relate."	
___ 11. "I've visited that home before, and found that both the mom and dad are trying very hard to help their son."	

<u>Skill Learning Activity 11.2 Observe and Analyze: Member Meeting Responsibilities (p. 263)</u>

Recall the last time you attended a small group problem-solving meeting. On a scale of 1 to 5 (1=not at all, 2=poorly, 3=somewhat, 4=well done, 5=to the best of my ability) rate yourself on how well you carried out each of the preparation, participation, and follow-up guidelines. Use the check sheet that follows. Analyze your responses and determine how effectively you participated in that meeting. What do you need to work on to become a more valuable member of a problem-solving group? Why? Write a paragraph in which you describe what you have learned. Additional copies of the check sheet are available at the Communicate! web site.

Member Meeting Responsibilities Rating Check Sheet

Instructions: Recall the last small group problem solving meeting you attended. Use the following scale to rate how well you carried out each of the member responsibilities.

1 = not at all   2 = poorly   3 = somewhat   4 = mostly   5 = to the best of my ability

Preparing

_____ 1. Studied the agenda

_____ 2. Studied the minutes

_____ 3. Prepared for your contributions

_____ 4. Prepared to play a major role

_____ 5. Listed questions

_____ *Total for preparation*

Participating

_____ 1. Listened attentively

_____ 2. Stayed focused

_____ 3. Asked questions

_____ 4. Took notes

_____ 5. Played devil's advocate

_____ 6. Monitored your contributions

_____ *Total for participation*

Following up

_____ 1. Reviewed and summarized your notes

_____ 2. Evaluated your effectiveness

_____ 3. Reviewed decisions

_____ 4. Communicated progress

_____ 5. Followed up

_____ 6. Reviewed minutes

_____ *Total for follow-up*

_____ **Total for preparation, participation, and follow-up**

Skill Learning Activity 11.3 Observe and Analyze: Emerging Informal Leadership in CBS's *Survivor* Series (p. 265)

Watch an early episode in of one of the popular CBS *Survivor* series (for example, Amazon or Outback). Select one tribe and identify the dominant roles that each member of the group seems to play in that episode. Use your Communicate! CD-ROM to access Skill Learning Activity 11.3 which provides a link to the web site for each *Survivor* series. Use the "episode" recap to help you in your analysis. Who is vying for informal leadership? How are they trying to gain or maintain their leadership? Explain what you think will happen to each leader candidate. Then on the web site for the *Survivor* series you have chosen, see how well your predictions held up. Write a short essay describing what you have learned.

Skill Learning Activity 11.4 Conversation and Analysis: Group Communication (p. 272)
Use you Communicate! CD ROM to access the video clip of the Student Government Financial Committee meeting. Click on the "In Action" icon in the menu on the left, then click on "Conversation menu" in the menu bar. Select Group Communication to watch the video (it takes a minute for the video to load). As you watch the conversation, observe the group's dynamics. Is their goal clear? Do they have sufficient diversity in their membership? What stage of group development do they appear to be in? Are they using the problem-solving method? What roles are being played by each member? Do they appear to be prepared for the meeting? You can answer these and other analysis questions by clicking "Analysis" in the menu bar at the top of the screen. When you've answered all the questions, click "Done" to compare your answers with the models provided by the authors. Printed below is a transcript of the meeting. You can also find this transcript online at the Communicate! web site.

Note: As members of the Student Government Financial Committee, Davinia, Joyce, Thomas, and Pat make decisions on how much funding, if any, to give to various student groups that request support from the funds collected from student fees. They are meeting for the first time in a campus cafeteria.

Conversation	**Analysis**
Thomas: Well, we've got twenty-three applications for funding and a total of $19,000 that we can distribute.	_____ _____ _____
Davinia: Maybe we should start by listing how much each of the twenty-three groups wants.	_____ _____

Joyce: It might be better to start by determining the criteria that we will use to decide if groups get any funding from student fees.

Davinia: Yeah, right. We should set up our criteria before we look at applications.

Thomas: Sounds good to me. Pat, what do you think?

Pat: I'm on board. Let's set up criteria first and then review the applications against those.

Joyce: Okay, we might start by looking at the criteria used last year by the Financial Committee. Does anyone have a copy of those?

Thomas: I do. *(He passes out copies to the other three people.)* They had three criteria: service to a significant number of students, compliance with the college's nondiscrimination policies, and educational benefit.

Davinia: What counts as "educational benefit"? Did last year's committee specify that?

Joyce: Good question. Thomas, you were on the committee last year. Do you remember what they counted as educational benefit?

Thomas: The main thing I remember is that it was distinguished from artistic benefit——like a concert or art exhibit or something like that.

a concert or art exhibit or something like that.

Pat: But can't art be educational?

Davinia: Yeah, I think so. Thomas, Joyce, do you?

Thomas: I guess, but it's like art's primary purpose isn't to educate.

Joyce: I agree. It's kind of hard to put into words, but I think educational benefit has more to do with information and the mind, and art has more to do with the soul. Does that sound too hokey?

Laughter.

Pat: Okay, so we want to say that we don't distribute funds to any hokey groups, right?

More laughter.

Davinia: It's not like we're against art or anything. It's just the funding we can distribute is for educational benefit, right?

Everyone nods.

Joyce: Okay, let's move onto another criterion. What is the significant number of students?

Thomas: Last year we said that the proposals for using money had to be of potential interest to at least 20 percent of students to get funding. How does that sound to you?

Pat: Sounds okay as long as we remember that something can be of potential interest to students who aren't members of specific groups. Like, for instance, I might want to attend a program on Native American customs even though I'm not a Native American. See what I mean?

Davinia: Good point——we don't want to define student interest as student identity or anything like that.

Nods of agreement.

Thomas: Okay, so are we agreed that 20 percent is about right with the understanding that the 20% can include students who aren't in a group applying for funding? *(Nods.)* Okay, then do we need to discuss the criterion of compliance with the college's policies on nondiscrimination?

_____
_____
_____
_____
_____
_____
_____
_____
_____
_____
_____
_____
_____
_____
_____
_____
_____
_____

Skill Learning Activity 11.5 Test Your Competence: Consulting on Meeting Effectiveness (p. 274)

If you are part of an on-going task group in this class use this group to complete this activity. If you are not in an on-going task group in this class, follow your instructor's directions for identifying an appropriate group to use for this activity. You are to act as a consultant to your group by evaluating the last meeting (or the next meeting) of your group using the decision effectiveness, participation and role behavior, and leader behavior rating sheets. Based on your ratings, write a short consultant's report in which you identify the group's strengths and weaknesses. Then develop five to seven specific action recommendations for improving the next meeting of the group. You can print out copies of the rating sheets, write, and submit your report to your instructor by e-mail at the Communicate! web site. Copies of the Group Effectiveness Rating Sheet, the Participation and Role Behavior Rating Sheet, and the Leader Behavior Rating Sheet also appear on the pages that follow.

Group Effectiveness Rating Sheet

Rate the group as a whole on each of the following questions using the following scale.

1 = always   2 = often   3 = sometimes   4 = rarely   5 = never

Group characteristics

_____ 1. Did the group have a clearly defined goal to which most members were committed?

_____ 2. Did the group's size fit the tasks required to meet its goals?

_____ 3. Was group-member diversity sufficient to ensure that important viewpoints were expressed?

_____ 4. Did group cohesiveness aid in task accomplishment?

_____ 5. Did group norms help accomplish goals and maintain relationships?

_____ 6. Was the physical setting conducive to accomplishing the work?

Member relationships

_____ 1. Did members feel valued and respected by others?

_____ 2. Were members comfortable interacting with others?

_____ 3. Did members balance speaking time so that all members participated?

_____ 4. Were conflicts seen as positive experiences?

_____ 5. Did members like and enjoy each other?

Group problem-solving

_____ 1. Did the group take time to define its problem?

_____ 2. Was high-quality information presented to help the group understand the problem?

_____ 3. Did the group develop criteria before suggesting solutions?

_____ 4. Were the criteria discussed sufficiently and based on all of the information available?

_____ 5. Did the group use effective brainstorming techniques to develop a comprehensive list of creative solution alternatives?

_____ 6. Did the group fairly and thoroughly compare each alternative to all solution criteria?

_____ 7. Did the group follow its decision rules in choosing among alternatives that met the criteria?

_____ 8. Did the group arrive at a decision that members agreed to support?

The Participation and Role Behavior Rating Sheet

Name of participant: _____

For each characteristic listed below, rate the participant on a scale of 1 to 5.

1 = excellent   2 = good   3 = average   4 = fair   5 = poor

Meeting behavior

_____ 1. Prepared and knowledgeable

_____ 2. Contributed ideas and opinions

_____ 3. Actively listened to the ideas of others

_____ 4. Politely voiced disagreement

_____ 5. Completed between-meeting assigned tasks

Performance of task-oriented roles

_____ 1. Acted as information or opinion giver

_____ 2. Acted as information seeker

_____ 3. Acted as analyzer

Performance of procedural roles

_____ 1. Acted as expediter

_____ 2. Acted as recorder

_____ 3. Acted as gatekeeper

Performance of maintenance roles

_____ 1. Acted as supporter

_____ 2. Acted as tension reliever

_____ 3. Acted as harmonizer

_____ 4. Acted as interpreter

Avoidance of self-centered roles

_____ 1. Avoided acting as aggressor

_____ 2. Avoided acting as joker

_____ 3. Avoided acting as withdrawer

_____ 4. Avoided acting as monopolizer

Qualitative Analysis

Based on the quantitative analysis above, write a two- to five-paragraph analysis of the person's participation. Be sure to give specific examples of the person's behavior to back up your conclusions.

Leader Behavior Rating Sheet

Was there a formal group leader?   Yes _____ No _____

If yes, name this person: _____

Who were the informal leaders of the group?

a. _____

b. _____

c. _____

Which of these leaders was most influential in helping the group meet its goals?

_____

Rate this leader on each of the following questions using a scale of 1 to 5:

1 = always   2 = often   3 = sometimes   4 = rarely   5 = never

_____ 1. Demonstrated commitment to the group and its goals.
_____ 2. Actively listened to ideas and opinions of others.
_____ 3. Adapted his or her behavior to the immediate needs of the group.
_____ 4. Avoided stating overly strong opinions.
_____ 5. Managed meaning for the group by framing issues and ideas.
_____ 6. Was prepared for all meetings.
_____ 7. Kept the group on task and on schedule.
_____ 8. Made sure that conflicts were handled effectively.
_____ 9. Implemented the group's decision rules effectively.
_____ 10. Worked to repair damaged relationships.
_____ 11. Followed up after meetings to see how members were progressing on assignments.

Activity 11.6 Using InfoTrac College Edition

Under the subject "leadership," click on "periodical references." Scroll to "Principles of Leadership," by Edward Moyers, July 15, 2000. Look for the heading "II: Leadership is not a popularity contest," and find the statement "Respect is what a true leader strives for – not just to be liked by all the people you are involved with." Of the eight ways of earning respect, which one or two do you believe it is most important to put into practice? Why?

Activity 11.7 Using InfoTrac College Edition
What does it take to be an effective leader? Under the subject "leadership," click on "periodical references." Scroll to "Lead, follow, or get out of the way," by Marcia A. Reed-Woodard, April 2001. What does the author say about the importance of knowing the people you are leading? Summarize the article below.

Activity 11.8 Thinking about Roles
Which of the three types of positive roles (task, maintenance, procedural) discussed do you perform the most frequently when you are in a group? Which do you perform the least frequently? Which role is easiest for you to perform? Which role is most difficult for you? Why? Do you ever enact any of the self-centered roles? If so, which ones? Do you see why these roles hurt the effectiveness of the group? How can you eliminate these behaviors?

Activity 11.9 What Would You Do? A Question of Ethics (p. 276)
Read the *What Would You Do: A Question of Ethics* scenario on page 276 of your text. Answer the following questions in the space provided here.

1. Should Sue follow Heather's advice? Why or Why not?

2. What would you do if you were in Heather's situation? What advice would you give Sue?

Web Resource 11.1: Identifying Your Team Player Style (p. 260)To see how you are likely to contribute to group or team effectiveness, use your Communicate! CD-ROM to access Web Resource 11.1: Identifying Your Team Player Style.

Web Resource 11.2: Taking Notes (p. 262)
For tips on how to take minutes in meetings, use your Communicate! CD-ROM to access Web Resource 11.2: Taking Notes.

Web Resource 11.3: Assert Yourself in Meetings (p. 260)
To read some about some useful steps for speaking out in meetings, use your Communicate! CD-ROM to access Web Resource 11.3: Assert Yourself in Meetings.

Web Resource 11.4: Dealing With Your Notes (p. 263)
For a detailed discussion of how to process your meeting notes, use your Communicate! CD-ROM to access Web Resource 11.4: Dealing With Your Notes.

Web Resource 11.5: Leadership Principles (p. 265)
To explore seven principles that are useful for maintaining leadership during difficult challenges, use your Communicate! CD-ROM to access Web Resource 11.5: Leadership Principles.

Web Resource 11.6: Scripting the Agenda (p. 268)
For ideas about agenda preparation, use your Communicate! CD-ROM to access Web Resource 11.6: Scripting the Agenda.

Chapter 11 Self-Test (answers and page references in Appendix)

True/False

1. A role is a specific pattern of behavior that one group member performs.

2. Information givers are people who probe the content and reasoning of members.

3. According to Bales, 16-26 percent of group time is typically spent on seeking information.

4. It is good to have jokers in a group as they help with tension relief.

5. It is possible for an individual to play more than one role in a group.

6. Devil's Advocate is a negative role to play in a group.

7. It is important for a leader to speak to group participants before the meeting.

Multiple Choice

1. Which of the following is *not* one of the four types of roles discussed in the text?
    a. task-related
    b. maintenance
    c. procedural
    d. other-centered
    e. self-centered

2. In a problem-solving group, Maria provides the group with data that helps it to make an effective decision. Maria's role can be described as
    a. information or opinion giver
    b. information or opinion seeker
    c. analyzer
    d. harmonizer

3. Carlos notices the group is in a lethargic, tense state. He tells a quick joke to get everyone to lighten up. Carlos is trying to be an effective
    a. interpreter
    b. harmonizer
    c. tension reliever
    d. maintainer
    e. expediter

4. Len has been appointed the chair of the committee in charge of selecting a new student representative to the governing board. He is what type of leader?
    a. informal
    b. formal
    c. charismatic
    d. framing

5. The process of influencing members to accomplish group goals is the definition of
    a. roles
    b. leadership
    c. maintenance
    d. framing

6. Which of the following is not one of the ways the effectiveness of a group is measured?
   a. The decision
   b. Individual participation and role behavior
   c. Leadership
   d. All of the above are ways to measure group effectiveness

7. Mark compliments Dana on the quality of her contribution by saying "Nice point Dana!" Mark is enacting what role at this time?
   a. harmonizer
   b. supporter
   c. gatekeeper
   d. monopolizer
   e. interpreter

8. Which of the following is not one of the activities a leader completes before the meeting?
   a. prepare the agenda
   b. arrange the time and place of the meeting
   c. review the agenda
   d. speak with each group participant

Essay

1. Discuss the differences between formal and informal leadership. Note differences in the areas of how one becomes a leader and how one maintains leadership.

2. What are some of the guidelines the text provides to assist leaders in making meetings more productive? Of all of these, which do you feel is the most important and why?

3. Review some of the text's recommendations for gaining influence and leadership.

4. Discuss the differences between task and maintenance roles. Why are maintenance roles important to effective groups?

5. Discuss the three ways we can evaluate the effectiveness of the group. Why is each important?

Helpful Links

http://www.motivation-tools.com/workplace/leadership_styles.htm - **Motivation and Leadership Styles**
This site, by Motivational Tools.com, explores the relationship between different styles of leadership and motivation

http://www.nwlink.com/~donclark/leader/leader.html - **Big Dog's Leadership Page**
By Don Clark, this site offers an overview of leadership styles and skills.

http://www.mapnp.org/library/ldrship/ldrship.htm - **Overview of leadership in Organizations**
Carter McNamara's site reviews leadership in the organization, covering topics such the difference between leading and managing, how to lead, and offering links to other resources.

http://www.teal.org.uk/styleind.htm - Check Out Your Own Leadership Style
This site allows you to take an online quiz to determine your style of leadership.

http://www.breakoutofthebox.com/ldrho.htm - **Leadership And The Enneagram**
A review of 9 different leadership styles by Mary R. Bast.

(See your Communicate! CD-ROM for links to other websites referenced in your text.)

IV

PUBLIC SPEAKING

CHAPTER 12: Determining Your Speaking Goal

Interactive Chapter Outline

I. Identifying Topics

_____

_____

  A. Listing Subjects

_____

_____

  B. Brainstorming for Potential Topics

_____

_____

II. Analyzing the Audience

_____

_____

  A. Kinds of Audience Data Needed

_____

_____

B. Ways of Gathering Data

_____

_____

    1. _____

    2. _____

    3. _____

C. Using Audience Analysis to Forecast Audience Reactions

_____

_____

    1. Audience knowledge

    _____

    2. Audience Interest

    _____

    3. Audience attitude toward your subject

    _____

    4. Audience attitude toward you as a speaker

    _____

III. Understanding the Speech Setting

_____

1. _____

2. _____

3. _____

4. _____

5. _____

6. _____

7. _____

IV. Selecting the Topic

_____

_____

V. Developing a Specific Speech Goal

A. General and Specific Goals

_____

_____

B. Phrasing a Specific Speech Goal

_____

_____

1. _____

2. _____

3. _____

4. _____

Key Terms

subject (p. 283)

_____

_____

topic (p. 283)

_____

_____

brainstorming (p. 284)

_____

_____

audience analysis (p. 285)

_____

_____

audience adaptation (p. 286)

_____

_____

credibility (p. 289)

_____

_____

setting (p. 290)

_____

_____

general speech goal (p. 294)

_____

_____

specific goal (p. 294)

_____

_____

Exercises

Skill Building Activity 12.1 Action Step 1.a: Brainstorm for Topics (p. 285)

1. Divide a sheet of paper into three columns. Label column 1 with your major or vocation such as "Art History"; label column 2 with a hobby or an activity, such as "Chess"; and label column 3 with a concern or an issue, such as "Water Pollution."
2. Working on one subject column at a time, quickly brainstorm a list of at least fifteen related topics for each column.
3. Place a check mark next to the three topics in each list that you would most enjoy speaking on.
4. Keep these lists for future use in choosing a topic for an assigned speech.

You can complete this complete this activity on line at the Communicate! web site, print it, or e-mail it to your instructor. You may also use the worksheet on the next page.

Brainstorming Worksheet

Vocation or major	Hobby or activity	Concern or interest
☐	☐	☐
☐	☐	☐
☐	☐	☐
☐	☐	☐
☐	☐	☐
☐	☐	☐
☐	☐	☐
☐	☐	☐
☐	☐	☐
☐	☐	☐
☐	☐	☐
☐	☐	☐
☐	☐	☐
☐	☐	☐
☐	☐	☐
☐	☐	☐
☐	☐	☐
☐	☐	☐

Skill Building Activity 12.2 Action Step 1.b: Analyzing Your Audience (p. 290)

1. Fill in the checklist, including subject, data about your classroom audience, and predictions about their reactions to your subject.

2. Make sure that you have completed the "because" part of each of the four predictions.

3. Save the results. You will use the data from this checklist throughout the preparation process.

At the Communicate! web site you can complete this activity, print it, and e-mail it to your instructor. On line, you can also view a sample of the Audience Analysis checklist prepared by a student in a similar course.

Audience Analysis Checklist

Subject _____

Data

1. The average audience member's education level is _____ high school _____ college _____ postgraduate.

2. The ages of the audience range from _____ to _____. The average age is about _____.

3. The audience is approximately _____ percent male and _____ female.

4. My estimate of the average socioeconomic level of the audience is _____ low _____ middle _____ high.

5. Most audience members are _____ of the same occupation/major _____ of different occupations/majors

6. The audience members are _____ mostly of the same race _____ a mixture of races.

7. The audience members are _____ mostly of the same ethnicity _____ a mixture of ethnicities.

8. The audience members are _____ mostly practice the same religion _____ practice a mixture of religions.

9. Most audience members are from the same _____ country _____ state _____ city _____ neighborhood.

10. Most audience members speak _____ the same first language _____ different first languages _____ English as a common language _____ some other common language (*list them:* _____).

Predictions based on audience data

1. Audience knowledge of the subject will be _____ extensive _____ moderate _____ limited because _____ .

2. Audience interest in this subject is likely to be _____ high _____ moderate _____ low because _____ .

3. Audience attitude toward my subject is likely to be _____ positive _____ neutral _____ negative because _____ .

4. My initial credibility with the audience is likely to be _____ high _____ medium _____ low because _____ .

Skill Building Activity 12.3 Action Step 1.c: Understanding the Speech Setting (p. 292)

1. Use the Setting checklist below to collect information about your occasion and location of your speech.
2. Write a short statement indicating which of these seem most important to your speech preparation? Why?
3. Save the results. You will use the data from this checklist throughout the preparation process.

At the Communicate! web site you can complete this activity, print it, and e-mail it to your instructor. On line, you can also view a sample of the Setting Analysis prepared by a student in a similar course.

Setting Checklist

Topic: _____

1. When will the speech be given? _____

2. Where in the program does the speech occur? _____

3. How large will the audience be? _____

4. Where in the program does the speech occur? _____

5. What is the time limit for the speech? _____

6. What is the layout of the room? _____

_____

7. What equipment is necessary to give the speech? _____

Skill Building Activity 12.4 Action Step 1.d: Selecting a Topic (p. 293)
1. Review the three topics that you checked from each of the lists of topics that you Brainstormed during Activity 1.a., the Audience Analysis you completed during Activity 1.b, and the Setting Checklist you completed during Activity 1.c.

2. From the three categories in the Brainstorming list, select the subject area that you want to use for your first speech.

3. Now select which of the three topics that you checked that you think would be of greatest benefit to your audience.

You can also complete this exercise online at the Communicate! web site.

Topic Selection Worksheet

Vocation or major	Hobby or activity	Concern or interest
☐	☐	☐
☐	☐	☐
☐	☐	☐
☐	☐	☐
☐	☐	☐
☐	☐	☐
☐	☐	☐
☐	☐	☐
☐	☐	☐
☐	☐	☐
☐	☐	☐

□	□	□
□	□	□
□	□	□
□	□	□

My topic will be _____

Skill Building Activity 12.5 Observe and Analyze: Recognizing a Specific Goal (p. 295)
Access InfoTrac College Edition and search with the journal name (jn) "Vital Speeches".
Find a speech on a topic that interests you. Then read that speech in order to identify
the speaker's goal. Was the goal clearly stated in the introduction? Was it implied but
clear? Was it unclear? Note how this analysis can help you clarify your own speech
goal. Write a paragraph explaining what you have learned.

Skill Building Activity 12.6 Action Step 1.e: Writing a Specific Goal (p. 297)
Write a specific goal for your first major speech.

Type of speech? _____

1. Write a first draft of your speech goal using a complete sentence that specifies
    the type response you want from the audience:

2. Test the infinitive. Does is express the kind of speech you are assigned to
    present? If not, write a revised infinitive:

3. Review the stated goal. If the statement contains more than one idea, revise
    the sentence so that the goal contains only one idea:

4. Test the infinitive phrase. Does the infinitive phrase express precisely the
    specific audience reaction desired? If not revise the infinitive phrase:

Write your final wording of the specific goal that you will use in your speech:

_____

_____

_____

At the Communicate! web site you will be directed to Speech Builder Express, a step-by-step program that will help you develop your speech as you work through each of the action steps.

Activity 12.7 Using InfoTrac College Edition

Using the same InfoTrac College Edition search as in activity 12.5, select a speech on a topic that at first glance does not seem interesting to you, but that you think may be relevant to you in some way. Read that speech. When you are done, answer the following questions in the space provided below: After reading the speech, did you find it more interesting than you originally thought? Why? What did the speaker do to try and draw you into the topic, or make the topic seem more interesting or relevant than you originally thought it would be? Note how this analysis can help you as you prepare your own speeches as you strive to relate your speech topic to your audience.

Activity 12.8 Audience Attitude Toward Your Topic

There are many organizations that poll public opinion on topics. If you have no idea about how your specific audience might react to your topic, you may be able to find some idea of general attitudes by accessing public opinion polls. The following web sites are good places to look for opinion polls:

http://www.WashingtonPost.com (Click on "Politics," then "Polls")
http://www.pollingreport.com
http://www.gallup.com

Visit each of these sites and examine the polling data available. These may be useful for your speeches. Use the space below for notes.

Activity 12.9 What Would You Do? A Question of Ethics (p. 298)

Read the *What Would You Do: A Question of Ethics* scenario on page 298 of your text. Answer the following questions in the space provided here.

1. What is the ethical issue at stake?

2. Was there anything about Glen's behavior that was unethical? Anything about Adam's?

3. What should be the penalty, if any, for Glen? For Adam?

Activity 12.10 From the Audience's Perspective
Using the Audience Analysis Checklist form from activity 12.2 and a partner, analyze a speech topic from the perspective of the audience. Have a partner from your class provide you with his/her speech topic and specific speech goal. As an audience member, how would you react to this speech? Fill out the "Predictions" portion of the Audience Analysis Checklist found in 12.2 accordingly. Your partner will be doing the same for your speech. After both of you have completed the forms, exchange them. How is the form you filled out in activity 12.2 for your speech different from the one your partner just filled out? If there are differences, how might they affect the preparation of your speech? (You may print out fresh copies of the checklist at the Communicate! web site.)

Web Resource 12.1: Brainstorming (p. 284)
For additional information on brainstorming, use your Communicate! CD-ROM to access Web Resource 12.1: Brainstorming.

Web Resource 12.2: Defining Your Audience (p. 286)
To read an interesting article on the importance of careful audience analysis, use your Communicate! CD-ROM to access Web Resource 12.2: Defining Your Audience.

Web Resource 12.3: Public Opinion Polls (p. 2886)
To access links to two respected polling organizations, use your Communicate! CD-ROM to access Web Resource 12.3: Public Opinion Polls.

Chapter 12 Self-Test (answers and page references in Appendix)

True/False

1. Topic and Subject are the same thing in public speaking.

2. "A broad area of knowledge" is the definition of a topic.

3. Personal observation can be a useful method of gathering data about an audience.

4. You will be less likely to be able to move about when the audience is much larger than approximately 50 people.

5. Most speeches can be classified as speeches that are meant to persuade, inform or entertain.

6. The specific goal is a single statement of the exact response the speaker wants from the audience.

7. As you speeches will be at least several minutes long, it is acceptable for speech goal statements to encompass several broad ideas.

Multiple Choice

1. The method for generating topics discussed in the text is called
   a. brainstorming
   b. analyzing
   c. adapting
   d. recording

2. The sentence: "I want the audience to understand the procedure for registering for classes at the college" is an example of
   a. general speech goal
   b. thesis statement
   c. specific speech goal
   d. topic sentence

e. none of the above

3. The size of the audience
   a. has no bearing on speech preparation
   b. may limit how much you are able to move around
   c. may require you to wear a microphone
   d. b and c

4. Tiffany is sitting in the class she will be giving a speech to in the future. She looks around the room, noting the average age of her classmates, their gender and ethnic makeup. Tiffany is engaging in what practice?
   a. group affiliation
   b. uniqueness
   c. brainstorming
   d. gathering audience data by observation

5. Antwon is analyzing his audience. Which of the following should he *not* consider when doing this?
   a. audience attitude toward the speaker
   b. audience attitude toward the setting
   c. audience attitude toward the topic
   d. audience interest in the topic
   e. all are discussed in the text as important to consider

6. Which of the following is not a common general speech goal?
   a. to analyze
   b. to entertain
   c. to inform
   d. to persuade
   e. all are common general goals

7. What is wrong with the following specific speech goal?
   "I want my audience to understand why dyslexia is a problem to children and to adults."
   a. This goal is a complete sentence
   b. This goal contains two distinct ideas.
   c. This goal is not for an informative speech
   d. There is nothing wrong with this specific speech goal

8. Which of the following statements best represents the difference between topic and subject?

a. subject is a broad area of knowledge while topic is a general aspect of subject.
b. subject is more specific than topic
c. subject is a broad area while topic is a specific aspect of subject
d. topic and subject are synonymous

Essay

1. Why is it important to know about your audience before you give a speech?

2. Why is it important to have a clear speech goal? Discuss this from the perspective of both audience and speaker.

3. Discuss the different ways of gathering audience data.

4. What is the importance of understanding the speech setting?

5. How can we use demographic data abut an audience to forecast the audience's reaction to a subject?

Helpful Links

http://www.public-speaking.org/public-speaking-articles.htm#topic – **Topic Development**
A series of articles on topic development from the Advanced Public Speaking Institute.

http://www.ukans.edu/cwis/units/coms2/vpa/vpa2.htm - **Selecting Your Topic**
Another site devoted to topic selection, this page is part of the University of Kansas' Virtual Presentation Assistant.

http://www.public-speaking.org/public-speaking-articles.htm - **Audience**
A few articles on the audience from the Advanced Public Speaking Institute.
http://www.toastmasters.org/ - **Toastmasters International**
The homepage for Toastmaster's International, an organization devoted to improving speaking skills.

http://www.ukans.edu/cwis/units/coms2/vpa/vpa1.htm - **Determining Your Purpose**
The University of Kansas' Virtual Presentation Assistant provides help with determining the purpose of your speech.

http://www.pollingreport.com – **Polling Report.com**
Contains lists of public polling results and information on public opinion research.

http://www.gallup.com – **The Gallup Organization**
Gallup is an organization devoted to research on public opinion. Much polling data can be found at their extensive web site.

(See your Communicate! CD-ROM for links to other websites referenced in your text.)

CHAPTER 13: Doing Research

- What sources of information are commonly used in preparing speeches and how can you find them?
- How can you evaluate information sources?
- What types of information are useful for developing speeches?
- What is the difference between fact and opinion statements?
- How are different types of information used in developing a speech?
- Why should you use the note card system for recording information items?
- What should be included on a note card?
- How do you verbally cite the sources of the information items you use in a speech?

Interactive Chapter Outline

I. Locate and Evaluate Information Sources

_____

_____

   A. Personal Knowledge, Experience, and Observation

_____

_____

   B. Books, Articles and General References

_____

_____

      1. Books _____

_____

2. Articles _____

_____

3. Newspapers _____

_____

4. Encyclopedias _____

_____

5. Statistical sources _____

_____

6. Biographical references _____

_____

7. Books of quotations _____

_____

8. United States government publications _____

_____

C. Internet Resources

_____

_____

1. Hosted Web sites _____

_____

2. Personal Web pages _____

_____

D. Surveys

_____

_____

E. Interviews

_____

_____

F. Skimming to Determine Source Value

_____

_____

G. Criteria for Judging Sources

_____

_____

    1. _____

    2. _____

    3. _____

II. Identify and Select Relevant Information

_____

_____

A. Factual Statements

_____

_____

1. Factual Statements _____

_____

2. Examples _____

_____

3. Statistics _____

_____

_____

_____

B. Expert Opinion

_____

_____

C. Elaborations

_____

_____

1. Anecdotes and Narratives _____

_____

2. Comparisons and Contrasts _____

_____

3. Quotations _____

_____

D. Drawing Information from Multiple Cultural Perspectives

_____

_____

E. Recording Information and Citing Written and Electronic Sources

_____

_____

A. Recording Data

_____

_____

III. Preparing to Cite Sources in the Speech

_____

_____

_____

_____

Key Terms

electronic database (p. 307)

_____

_____

periodicals (p. 308)

_____

_____

Internet (p. 311)

_____

_____

newsgroup or bulletin board (p. 312)

_____

_____

survey (p. 313)

_____

_____

skimming (p. 314)

_____

_____

factual statements (p. 317)

_____

_____

examples (p. 317)

_____

_____

hypothetical examples (p. 317)

_____

_____

statistics (p. 318)

_____

_____

expert opinions (p. 319)

_____

_____

anecdotes (p. 319)

_____

_____

narratives (p. 319)

_____

_____

comparisons (p. 320)

_____

_____

contrasts (p. 321)

_____

_____

plagiarism (p. 321)

_____

_____

Exercises

<u>Skill Learning Activity 13.1 Action Step 2.a: Identify Potential Sources (p. 316)</u>
The goal of this activity is to help you compile a *list* of potential sources for your speech.

1. Identify gaps in your current knowledge that you would like to fill.

2. Identify a person, or an event, or a process that you could observe to broaden your personal knowledge base.

3. Brainstorm a list of key words that are related to your speech goal.

4. Work with paper or electronic versions of your library's card catalog, periodical indexes (including InfoTrac College Edition), and general references discussed in this chapter, find and list specific resources that appear to provide information for your speech.

5. Use a search engine, identify Internet sponsored and personal web sites that may be sources of information for your speech.

6. Identify a person you could interview for additional information for this speech.

7. Skim the resources you have identified to decide which are likely to be most useful.

8. Evaluate each resource to determine how much faith you can place in the information.

You may complete this activity on line at the Communicate! web site and view a student sample.

Skill Learning Activity 13.2 Action Step 2.b: Identify, Select and Record Relevant Information Items (p. 325)
The goal of this activity is to review the source material that you identified in Action Step 2.a and record specific items of information that you might wish to use in your speech.

1. Carefully read all print and electronic sources (including web material) that you have identified and evaluated as appropriate sources for your speech. Review your notes and tapes from all interviews and observations.

2. As you read an item (fact, opinion, example, illustration, statistic, anecdote, narrative, comparison/contrast, quotation, definition, or description) that you think might be useful in your speech, record the item on a 3x5 note card or on the appropriate online note card form for this activity, available at the Communicate! web site. (If you are using an article that originally appeared in a periodical but that you read online, use the periodical note card form.)

You can complete this activity on line at the Communicate! web site where you can view a sample of three note cards prepared by another student, use online forms to prepare your own electronic note cards, and print them out for use in preparing your speech. Paper copies of each note card appear below.

Electronic Note Card for a Book

Heading _____

Notes

_____

_____

_____

_____

_____

_____

Author(s) or editor(s) (last name, first name, middle initial)

_____

_____

_____

_____

_____

_____

Title _____

Page number(s) on which this item was found _____

Year of publication _____

Place of publication (city, state, or country) _____

Publishing company _____

Electronic Note Card for a Periodical

Heading _____

Notes

_____

_____

_____

_____

_____

_____

Author(s) (if listed) (last name, first name, middle initial)

_____

_____

_____

_____

_____

_____

Title of article _____

Title of periodical _____

Page number(s) of the article _____

Page number(s) on which this item was found _____

Day/month/year of publication (depending on periodical) _____

Volume number _____

Electronic Note Card for a Newspaper

Heading _____

Notes

_____

_____

_____

_____

_____

_____

Author(s) (if listed) (last name, first name, middle initial)

_____

_____

_____

_____

_____

_____

Title of article _____

Title of newspaper _____

Section number _____

Page number(s) of the article _____

Page number(s) on which this item was found _____

Day/month/year of publication _____

Electronic Note Card for a General Reference

Heading _____

Notes

_____

_____

_____

_____

_____

_____

Item author _____

Item/article title (if one is listed) _____

Volume author(s) or editors (s) (last name, first name, middle initial)

_____

_____

_____

_____

_____

_____

Reference title _____

Page number(s) on which this item was found _____

Year of publication _____

Place of publication (city, state, or country) _____

Publishing company _____

Electronic Note Card for a Web Site

Heading _____

Notes

_____

_____

_____

_____

_____

_____

Web address _____

Author(s) (last name, first name, middle initial)

_____

_____

_____

_____

_____

_____

Web page title (article) _____

Date of original posting _____

Date of most recent update _____

Electronic Note Card for an Interview

Heading _____

Notes

_____

_____

_____

_____

_____

_____

_____

Interviewee (last name, first name, middle initial) _____

Interviewee's title or qualifications _____

Interviewee's organizational affiliation _____

Date of interview _____

Place of interview (city, state, or country) _____

Title _____

Electronic Note Card for an Original Survey or Observation

Heading _____

Notes

_____

_____

_____

_____

_____

_____

_____

Place of survey or observation (city, state, or country)

_____

Date(s) of survey or observation _____

Description of people surveyed _____

Person, event, or process observed

Skill Learning Activity 13.3 Action Step 2.c: Prepare to Cite Your Sources (p. 326)
On the back of each note card you created in Action Step 2.b, write a short phrase you can use in your speech as a verbal citation for the material on that card.

Activity 13.4 Using InfoTrac College Edition
Use InfoTrac College Edition to find information on the subject you have selected for your speech. Click on periodical references. Look for articles that include information that seems relevant to your speech. Whether you download the article or make note cards, make sure that you have the necessary data to cite the source of information if you use it in your speech.

Activity 13.5 Using InfoTrac College Edition
Sometimes a search on your subject area may turn up few or no periodical references, or those that are returned do not contain information relevant to your specific purpose. What can be done in that case? Often times, a modified search may be more fruitful. Using InfoTrac College Edition, try modifying your search terms. For example, if you originally entered "decision making in small group communication," you may not have turned up many references. But if you entered "decision making" or "group communication," you will return many more periodical references. Try several different words and phrases related to your topic to return the most comprehensive list of results. Skim the articles that seem most relevant and save those that may be of use to you.

Activity 13.6 Using Technology
Online indexes and databases available through libraries as well as the Internet can be used to find sources for supporting material for your speeches. Check with your college or public library to see what indexes and databases you can access through them. For instance, using the Internet, you can access *The Statistical Abstract of the United States* at http://www.census.gov. As practice, visit the site and key in "U.S., crime, statistics." Spend a few minutes acquainting yourself with this site. How might you use this information in a speech on mandatory sentencing?

Activity 13.7 Using Technology – Library Orientation

Most college and university libraries maintain access to several electronic databases in addition to Internet access. In many cases, such as at small schools or community colleges, electronic databases may be the most robust sources of timely information available. In any cases, you will likely employ these resources to some extent. Call or drop by your circulation and reference desk to make an appointment with a librarian in order to receive an overview of what resources are available and instructions on their use. Many libraries have printed instructions as well and Internet-based tutorials as well. Practice using the resources available. Your research will be more efficient if you are knowledgeable in the use of various electronic databases. (Some libraries offer access to their electronic databases through their web pages as well.)

List the details of you library visit below if your instructor decides to make this activity a required component of the course.

Library Orientation Visit

Date/Time:

Name of Librarian:

List of electronic databases available:

Library website (if applicable):

Copies of printed instructions/web tutorial address obtained:

Activity 13.8 Using the Web

Search engines are not the only useful sources of information on the Internet. Most large media outlets and other sources of news and information have a presence on the Internet. Using the links provided in the "Useful and Interesting Internet Links" section of this chapter, search some media and reference resources for information on your topic. You may find further links, full text of articles and/or visual information such as graphics, photos or video. Take full notes, use the appropriate electronic note cards from Activity 13.2, download or print any relevant information you find. Be sure to compile full bibliographic information for citing your sources.

13.9 Quotations

Locate a book of quotations. *Bartlett's Familiar Quotations* is a popular example found in most libraries. Internet sites with similar information also exist. (See *Web Resource 13.4*) Skim through the book or browse the web site. Seek quotes relevant to your speech and write a few in the space below. How may these be used to enhance your speech? If quotations directly relevant to your topic are not found, how may a quote still be useful? What can it add to a speech? (Be sure to copy full bibliographic information concerning the source of the quote.)

13.10 What Would You Do? (p. 327)

Read the *What Would You Do: A Question of Ethics* scenario on page 327 of your text. Answer the following questions in the space provided here.

1. What do you think of Tom's assessment of his use of statistics that "No one is going to say anything about it"?

2. Does Tom have any further ethical obligation? If so, what is it?

Web Resource 13.1: Online Encyclopedias (p. 310)

For a list of encyclopedias that are available on the web, use your Communicate! CD-ROM to access Web Resource 13.1: Online Encyclopedias.

Web Resource 13.2: Online Encyclopedias (p. 310)

For links to web-based statistical sources, use your Communicate! CD-ROM to access Web Resource 13.2: Statistics Online.

Web Resource 13.3: Online Biographical References (p. 311)

For links to popular web-based biographical references, use your Communicate! CD-ROM to access Web Resource 13.3: Online Biographical References.

Web Resource 13.4: Quotations Online (p. 311)
For links to web-based collections of quotations, use your Communicate! CD-ROM to access Web Resource 13.4: Quotations Online.

Web Resource 13.5: Government Publications Online (p. 311)
For links to several frequently used U.S. federal government documents, use your Communicate! CD-ROM to access Web Resource 13.5: Government Publications Online.

Web Resource 13.6: Conducting Surveys (p. 313)
For important tips for collecting good information using surveys, use your Communicate! CD-ROM to access Web Resource 13.6: Conducting Surveys.

Web Resource 13.7: Analyzing Information Sources (p. 316)
To read about additional criteria you can use to evaluate your sources, use your Communicate! CD-ROM to access Web Resource 13.7: Analyzing Information Sources.

Chapter 13 Self-Test (answers and page references in Appendix)

True/False

1. Since note cards can be easily misplaced, they should not be used in speech research.

2. Personal knowledge and experience may be useful in a speech.

3. In order to not mislead your audience, use statistics that are both recent and older.

4. "Skimming" references should never be done as you can miss crucial details.

5. Objectivity of the source is not important when judging sources.

6. Factual statements can be verified.

7. Anecdotes are often amusing and generally brief stories.

Multiple Choice

1. Personal knowledge and experience
    a. are not valid sources of information for prepared speeches
    b. can be supplemented by careful observation
    c. can be useful if your topic is something you know about
    d. b and c
    e. none of the above

2. Which of these is not mentioned as a source of information for your speeches?
    a. personal experience
    b. books and articles
    c. your instructor
    d. United States government publications

3. If your topic is "in the news", which of the following is likely true:
    a. books will be better sources since they offer depth of information
    b. electronic databases will not be good sources as they are not current
    c. encyclopedias will likely be your only source of information
    d. periodicals will likely be your primary source of information as they are more current than books.

4. Interviews
    a. are not useful sources for speeches
    b. are best left to professionals
    c. can be very effective if you ask the right person good questions
    d. are great to use because they require no preparation

5. Expert opinions
    a. are judgments and interpretations made by authorities in a particular subject area.
    b. do not carry weight with any audiences
    c. can take the place of facts entirely
    d. are often more useful than facts

6. "The length of this aircraft carrier is equal to three and one half football fields." This statement is an example of a(n)
    a. contrast
    b. comparison
    c. statistic
    d. opinion

7. When citing sources in your speech
    a. it is best to put them all at the end of the speech

     b. audiences will better understand the depth of your research
     c. you should not include the date of the material
     d. there is no need to cite sources in the speech

8. Encyclopedias
     a. often can provide a good starting point for your research
     b. can be found online
     c. offer short articles on a variety of subjects
     d. all of the above are true.

Essay

1. Discuss what information should be placed on note cards? Why should note cards be used instead of a sheet or sheets of paper?

2. Why is it often important to draw sources from a variety of backgrounds?

3. Discuss the criteria for the evaluation of sources.

4. How can statistics be used as supporting information in a speech? Discuss the guidelines for effective use of statistics.

5. What are some of the most common sources of information used in speeches? Discuss the pros and cons of each.

Helpful Links

http://www.census.gov – **US Census Bureau Home Page**
This site compiles statistical data on the population of the United States. Much of it is derived from the most current census. Very useful for gathering statistical data on a wide range of topics.

http://www.yahoo.com – **Yahoo!**
A popular web search engine.

http://www.google.com – **Google**
Another search engine.

http://www.nytimes.com – **The New York Times**

The website for *The New York Times.* An excellent source for current information on national and world news. *The New York Times* is generally considered a "newspaper of record."

http://www.cnn.com – **CNN**
The website for Cable News Network, the 24 hour news cable television network. CNN presents a wide variety of national and international news, sports, weather and features and includes an archive of older material and links to related websites.

http://www.ukans.edu/cwis/units/coms2/vpa/vpa3.htm - **Researching Your Topic**
This link accesses research resources for speech writing provided by the University of Kansas' *Virtual Presentation Assistant.*

http://www.ipl.org/ - **Internet Public Library**
The Internet Public Library is exactly what it sounds like – an online reference collection.

http://www.loc.gov – **Library of Congress**
This link is the gateway to the Library of Congress. The Library of Congress is the largest library in the world, with more than 128 million items.

http://www.apastyle.org/elecref.html - **APA Style.org**
The American Psychological Association's guide to citing online sources.

http://webster.commnet.edu/mla/index.shtml# - **A Guide for Writing Research Papers**
Online guide to citing sources using the Modern language Association (MLA) format.

(See your Communicate! CD-ROM for links to other websites referenced in your text.)

CHAPTER 14: Organizing

Learning Objectives

After studying this chapter, you should be able to answer the following questions:

- How do you construct a thesis statement?
- How do you determine the main points for your speech?
- How do you determine the best order for your speech?
- What is the goal of transitions?
- What are the goals of an effective speech introduction?
- What are the most common types of speech introductions?
- What are the essentials of an effective speech conclusion?
- What are the major elements of a well-written speech outline?

Interactive Chapter Outline

I. Developing the Body of the Speech

_____

_____

   A. Writing a Thesis Statement

_____

_____

   B. Organizing and Outlining Main Points

_____

_____

      1. Write main points as complete sentences

_____

_____

      2. Revise main points

_____

_____

1) _____

2) _____

3) _____

4) _____

C. Ordering Main Points

_____

_____

   1. Topic order

_____

_____

   2. Time order

_____

_____

   3. Logical reasons order

_____

_____

D. Selecting and Outlining Supporting Material

_____

_____

    1. Developing supporting points

        _____

        _____

    2. Organize supporting material

        _____

        _____

  E. Planning and Outlining Section Transitions

_____

_____

IV. Preparing the Introduction

_____

_____

  A. Goals of the Introduction

_____

_____

    1. Getting attention

        _____

        _____

    2. Stating the thesis

        _____

3. Establishing your credibility

_____

_____

4. Setting a tone

_____

_____

5. Creating a bond of goodwill

_____

_____

B. Types of Introductions

_____

_____

1. Startling statement

_____

_____

2. Rhetorical question

_____

_____

3. Story

_____

_____

4. Personal reference

_____

_____

5. Quotation

_____

_____

6. Suspense

_____

_____

V. Creating the Conclusion

_____

_____

A. Summary

_____

_____

B. Story

_____

_____

C. Emotional Impact

thesis statement (p. 336)

main points (p. 338)

clear (p. 340)

parallel (p. 340)

meaningful (p. 341)

topic order (p. 342)

time (p. 343)

logical reasons order (p. 343)

transitions (p. 347)

_____

_____

section transitions (p. 347)

_____

_____

rhetorical question (p. 351)

_____

_____

appeal (p. 355)

_____

_____

Exercises

Skill Learning Activity 14.1 Action Step 3.a: Writing a Thesis Statement (p. 338)
The goal of this activity is to develop a well-worded thesis statement for your speech.

1. Write the specific goal you developed in Chapter 12 Speech Action Step Activity 1.e.

2. Does this specific speech goal list a specific number of main ideas?
3. If yes, list the ideas and move to item 6:

4. If no, based on your research, identify and list the specific ideas your audience must learn about if you are to reach the specific speech goal:

5. Review this list and identify items that can be grouped together under a larger category. Then select the two to five items that from your research you believe to be the most important for this audience to understand.

6. Now write a thesis statement that identifies your topic and previews these ideas.

You can also complete this activity online with Speech Builder Express, view a student sample of this activity, and, if required, email your completed activity to your instructor. Use your Communicate! CD-ROM to access Skill Learning Activity 14.1

Skill Learning Activity 14.2 Action Step 3.b: Organizing and Outlining the Main Points of Your Speech (p. 344)

The goal of this activity is to help you develop your main points.

1. Write your thesis statement:

2. Underline the 2-5 specific ideas identified in your thesis statement that you want to communicate to your audience in order to achieve your goal.

3. For each underlined item, write one sentence that summarizes what you want your audience to know about that idea.

4. Review the main points as a group.

    A. Are main points clear? If not consider why and revise.

    B Are the main points parallel in structure? If not consider why and revise.

    C Are the main points meaningful? If not consider why and revise.

5. Decide how to order these main points.

6. Write the main point statements in an order that will aid audience members in understanding your thesis and help you reach your goal.

You can also complete this activity online with Speech Builder Express, view a student sample of this activity, and, if required, email your completed activity to your instructor. Use your Communicate! CD-ROM to access Skill Learning Activity 14.2.

Skill Learning Activity 14.3 Action Step 3.c: Selecting and Outlining Supporting Material (p. 347)

The goal of this activity is to help you develop and outline your supporting material. Complete the following steps for each of your main points.

1. List the main point.

2. Using your note cards list the key information related to that main point that you uncovered during your research.

3. Analyze that information by crossing out information that seems less relevant, or doesn't fit.

4. Look for information that seems related and can be grouped under a broader heading.

5. Try to group information until you have between 2 and 4 supporting points.

6. Write the supporting points in full sentences.

7. Repeat this process for all main points.

8. Write an outline using Roman Numerals for main points, Capital letters for supporting points, and Arabic numbers for material related to supporting points.

You can also complete this activity online with Speech Builder Express, view a student sample of this activity, and, if required, email your completed activity to your instructor. Use your Communicate! CD-ROM to access Skill Learning Activity 14.3.

Skill Learning Activity 14.4 Action Step 3.d: Preparing Section Transitions (p. 349)
The goal of this exercise is to help you prepare section transitions. Section transitions appear as parenthetical statements before/after each main point. Using complete sentences:

1. Write a transition from your first main point to your second.

2. Write a transition from each of your remaining main points to the one before it.

3. Add these transitional statements to your outline.

You can also complete this activity online with Speech Builder Express, view a student sample of this activity, and, if required, email your completed activity to your instructor. Use your Communicate! CD-ROM to access Skill Learning Activity 14.4.

Skill Learning Activity 14.5 Action Step 3.e: Writing Speech Introductions   (p. 353)

The goal of this activity is to create several introductions so you have choices for how you will begin your speech.

1. For the speech body you outlined earlier, write three different types introductions for your speech chosen from these types: a startling statement, rhetorical question, story, personal reference, quotation, or suspense. Choose types that you believe would be appropriate for your speech goal and audience.

2. Of the three introductions you drafted, which do you believe is the best? Why?

3. Write that introduction in outline form.

You can also complete this activity online with Speech Builder Express, view a student sample of this activity, and, if required, email your completed activity to your instructor. Use your Communicate! CD-ROM to access Skill Learning Activity 14.5.

Skill Learning Activity 14.6 Action Step 3.f: Creating Speech Conclusions   (p. 356)

The goal of this activity is to help you create choices for how you will conclude your speech.

1. For the speech body you outlined earlier, write three different conclusions (summary, story, appeal to action, or emotional impact) that review important points you want the audience to remember and leave the audience with vivid imagery or an emotional appeal.

2. Which do you believe is the best? Why?

3. Write that conclusion in outline form.

You can also complete this activity online with Speech Builder Express, view a student sample of this activity, and, if required, email your completed activity to your instructor. Use your Communicate! CD-ROM to access Skill Learning Activity 14.6.

278

Skill Learning Activity 14.7 Action Step 3.g: Creating a Speech Source List (p. 357)
The goal of this activity is to help you record the list of sources you used in the speech.

1. Review your note cards, separating those whose information you have used in your speech from those you have not.

2. List the sources whose information was used in the speech by copying the bibliographic information recorded on the note card.

3. For short lists, organize your list alphabetically by the last name of the first author. Be sure to follow the form shown in Figure 14.2. If you did not record some of the bibliographic information on your note card, you will need to revisit the library or data base to find it.

You can also complete this activity online with Speech Builder Express, view a student sample of this activity, and, if required, email your completed activity to your instructor. Use your Communicate! CD-ROM to access Skill Learning Activity 14.7.

Skill Learning Activity 14.8 Action Step 3.h: Completing the Speech Outline (p. 360)
The goal of this activity is to write and review a complete sentence outline of the speech, using material you've developed so far with the action steps. You can also complete this activity online with Speech Builder Express, view a student sample of this activity, and, if required, email your completed activity to your instructor. Use your Communicate! CD-ROM to access Skill Learning Activity 14.8.

Activity 14.9 Using InfoTrac College Edition
Using InfoTrac College Edition, enter "Vital Speeches" in the journal name box. View Vital Speeches and identify three speeches to look at; then view those speeches. Read and analyze the introductions and conclusions to those speeches. Which ones meet the goals discussed in this chapter? What could the speakers have done to make the introductions and conclusions better? What qualities, if any, did you find helpful in preparing your introduction and conclusion?

Activity 14.10 Using InfoTrac College Edition
Using InfoTrac College Edition, enter "Vital Speeches" in the journal name box. Find the speech **Responding to the challenge: corporate governance**. Read the speech and attempt to develop a rough outline. What were the main ideas? Were transitions used? What strategies were employed in the introduction and conclusion? What changes, if any, would you make to the speech to make it easier to follow?

Activity 14.11 Using the Web
Locate a web site of quotations. Browse the site. Seek quotes relevant to your speech and write a few in the space below. How may these be used to enhance your introduction and/or conclusion? (Be sure to copy full bibliographic information concerning the source of the quote.)

Activity 14.12 What Would You Do? A Question of Ethics (p. 362)
Read the *What Would You Do: A Question of Ethics* scenario on page 362 of your text. Answer the following questions in the space provided here.

1. What are the ethical issues here?

2. Is anyone really hurt by Gloria opening the speech with this story?

3. What are the speaker's ethical responsibilities?

Web Resource 14.1: Writing Different Types of Thesis Statements (p. 338)

For guidance on writing analytical, expository, and persuasive thesis statements, use your Communicate! CD-ROM to access Web Resource 14.1: Writing Different Types of Thesis Statements.

Web Resource 14.2: Strategies for Introducing Speeches (p. 352)
For further discussion of speech introductions, use your Communicate! CD-ROM to access Web Resource 14.2: Strategies for Introducing Speeches.

Web Resource 14.3: Citation Styles (p. 356)
To view examples of common citations styled with the APA, *Chicago Manual of Style*, and AMA styles, use your Communicate! CD-ROM to access Web Resource 14.3: Citation Styles.

Chapter 14 Self Test (answers and page references in Appendix)

True/False

1. Transition statements should not be placed in the outline.

2. Topic order organizes the main ideas of a speech by categories or divisions.

3. Organizing the main points by steps in a process is called logical order.

4. Using a rhetorical question in the introduction is a poor idea because as the audience ponders the answer to the question, they will not be paying attention to the speech.

5. The appeal to action ends a persuasive speech.

6. Main points should contain one single idea.

7. An outline can easily contain almost as many words as the speech itself.

Multiple Choice

1. A thesis statement
   a. is a sentence that identifies the topic of your speech and the main ideas you will present

    b. is the same as the specific goal statement
    c. should be written after the introduction
    d. is not necessary in a well-organized speech

2. Main points should be
    a. clear
    b. written in parallel structure format
    c. limited to five or fewer in number
    d. meaningful
    e. all of the above

3. Daniel organizes his speech on changing the oil in a car with main ideas that are the steps in the process. His speech is organized using what order?
    a. time order
    b. logical reasons order
    c. problem-solution order
    d. topic order

4. At the end of her first main idea, Alexandra says: "Now that we have seen the causes of credit card debt, lets look at what we can do about it." You recognize this sentence as a:
    a. conclusion
    b. main point
    c. section transition
    d. attention getter
    e. none of the above

5. You are listening to a speech that starts off with the following: "What would you do if you won the lottery today? Would you spend the money? Would you save it? Would you donate it?" You recognize this as what type of introduction?
    a. startling statement
    b. rhetorical question
    c. reference
    d. emotional impact
    e. parallel structure

6. The two major goals of a speech conclusion are
    a. summarize and bond with the audience
    b. bond with the audience and emotionally impact the audience
    c. emotionally impact the audience and explain your thesis
    d. summarize and emotionally impact the audience

7. Listing sources
   a. is usually done alphabetically by author's last name
   b. will enable you to direct audience members to your sources
   c. can be done using a bibliographic style format such as APA or MLA
   d. all of the above

8. What is the problem with the following outline segment?

   I. Freshwater fishing requires certain pieces of equipment.
      A. A good-quality rod will help your casting.
      B. A properly constructed reel will help gain proper distance
      C. Fishing line of the right weight will allow you to catch larger fish
      D. Years of fishing experience also help.

   a. The main idea is written as a full sentence
   b. There are not enough subdivisions
   c. Subdivision D does not belong as "experience" is not a piece of equipment.
   d. There is nothing wrong with this outline segment

Essay

1. Discuss the several different goals of an introduction and at least three different ways of achieving those goals.

2. What are three different ways of organizing a speech and provide an example of each.

3. What are the four main types of conclusions and what are their main objectives?

4. What are transitions and why is it important to include them in speeches? Provide examples to illustrate your points.

5. What is a thesis statement and what purpose does it serve in speech preparation.

Helpful Links

http://www.public-speaking.org/public-speaking-articles.htm#organization –
Organization
A set of articles on organization from the Advanced Public Speaking Institute.
http://www.ukans.edu/cwis/units/coms2/vpa/vpa6.htm - **Tips on Outlining**
Tips on outlining from the Virtual Presentation Assistant of the University of Kansas.

_____

_____

D. Appeal to Action

_____

_____

VI. Listing Sources

_____

_____

VII. Completing the Outline

_____

_____

1. _____

2. _____

3. _____

4. _____

5. _____

Key Terms

organizing (p. 336)

_____

_____

speech outline (p. 336)

_____

http://www2.volstate.edu/humanities/comm/outlining/103inftime.htm
http://www2.volstate.edu/humanities/comm/outlining/103inftopical.htm
http://www2.volstate.edu/humanities/comm/outlining/103perlogicalreasons.htm -

Outline Design Guides
These three links provide access to sample outline "templates" for time order, topic order and logical reasons order speeches. They can be useful in visualizing an outline for these types of speeches. From Volunteer State Community College.
http://www.public-speaking.org/public-speaking-articles.htm#openings – **Openings**
A set of articles on openings (introductions) from the Advanced Public Speaking Institute.

http://www.public-speaking.org/public-speaking-articles.htm#closings – **Closings**
An article on closings (conclusions) from the Advanced Public Speaking Institute.

(See your Communicate! CD-ROM for links to other websites referenced in your text.)

CHAPTER 15: Adapting Verbally and Visually

- What can you do to develop common ground?
- What can you do to create or build audience interest?
- What can you do to adapt to your audience's knowledge and sophistication?
- What can you do to build the audience's perception of you as a speaker?
- What can you do to reinforce or change an audience's attitude toward your topic?
- What criteria do you use to select and construct visual aids?
- What do you include in an audience adaptation strategy?

Interactive Chapter Outline

I. Verbally Adapting to your Audience

_____

_____

   A. Establishing Common Ground

_____

_____

      1. Use personal pronouns

_____

_____

      2. Ask rhetorical questions

_____

_____

3. Share common experiences

_____

_____

4. Personalize information

_____

_____

B. Building and Maintaining Audience Interest

_____

_____

   1. Timeliness

_____

_____

   2. Proximity

_____

_____

   3. Seriousness

_____

_____

II. Adapting to the Audience's Knowledge and Sophistication

_____

_____

A. Orienting Listeners

_____

_____

B. Presenting New Information

_____

_____

    1. _____

    2. _____

    3. _____

    4. _____

III. Building Speaker Credibility

_____

_____

A. Knowledge and Expertise

_____

_____

B. Trustworthiness

_____

_____

C. Personableness

_____

_____

IV. Adapting to the Attitudes Toward Your Speech Goal

_____

_____

V. Adapting to Audiences from Different Cultures and Language Communities

_____

_____

VI. Adapting to Audiences Visually

_____

_____

    A. Types of Visual Aids

        1. Objects

_____

_____

        2. Models

_____

_____

        3. Still photographs

_____

_____

4. Slides

_____

_____

5. Film and video clips

_____

_____

6. Simple drawings

_____

_____

7. Maps

_____

8. Charts

_____

_____

9. Graphs

_____

_____

1) _____

2) _____

3) _____

B. Methods for Displaying Visual Aids

_____

_____

    1. Computer-mediated presentation

    _____

    _____

    2. Overhead transparencies

    _____

    _____

    3. Flipcharts

    _____

    _____

    4. Poster boards

    _____

    _____

    5. Chalkboard

    _____

    _____

    6. Handouts

    _____

    _____

C. Criteria for Choosing Visual Aids

_____

_____

1. _____

2. _____

3. _____

4. _____

5. _____

6. _____

VII. Principles for Creating Effective Visual Aids

_____

_____

1. _____

2. _____

3. _____

4. _____

5. _____

6. _____

7. _____

8. _____

Key Terms

audience adaptation (p. 368)

_____

_____

common ground (p. 368)

_____

_____

personal pronouns (p. 368)

_____

_____

rhetorical questions (p. 369)

_____

_____

personalize (p. 370)

_____

_____

timely (p. 372)

_____

_____

proximity (p. 372)

_____

_____

serious (p. 373)

_____

_____

credibility (p. 376)

_____

_____

knowledge and expertise (376)

_____

_____

trustworthiness (p. 376)

_____

_____

personableness (p. 377)

_____

_____

attitude (p. 378)

_____

_____

visual aids (p. 382)

_____

_____

chart (p. 385)

_____

_____

word chart (p. 385)

_____

flow chart (p. 386)

_____

graph (p. 386)

_____

bar graph (p. 386)

_____

line graph (p. 387)

_____

pie graph (p. 387)

_____

flip chart (p. 389)

_____

Exercises

Skill Learning Activity 15.1 Observe and Analyze: Creating Common Ground (p. 370)
Use your CD-Rom to access InfoTrac College Edition and search for the article "A Question of Real American Black Men," by Bailey B. Baker, Jr., *Vital Speeches*, April 15, 2002. Analyze how this speaker used use personal pronouns, rhetorical questions, common experiences, and personalized information to create common ground. Write a short essay describing the conclusions of your analysis.
You can complete this activity online and, if required, email it to your instructor. Use your Communicate! CD-ROM to access Skill Learning Activity 15.1

Skill Learning Activity 15.2 Action Step 4.a: Adapting to Your Audience Verbally (p. 381)
The goal of this activity is to help you plan how you will adapt your material to the specific audience verbally.

Write your thesis statement: _____

Review the audience analysis that you completed in Action Steps 1.b and 1.c. As you review your speech outline that you completed in Action Step 3.h, plan the specific tactics you will use to adapt this material to your audience by answering the following questions:

1. What are the key aspects of your audience that you will need to adapt to?

2. What will you do to establish and maintain common ground?

3. What will you do to build and maintain interest?

4. What will you do to increase audience understanding and retention?

5.   What will you do to build and maintain your credibility?

You can complete this activity online, view another student sample of this activity, and, if required, email your completed activity to your instructor. Use your Communicate! CD-ROM to access Skill Learning Activity 15.2.

Skill Learning Activity 15.3 Action Step 4.b: Adapting to Your Audience Visually (p. 392)
The goal of this activity is help you decide what visual aids you will use in your speech.

1. Identify the key ideas in you speech that you believe a visual presentation would increase audience interest, understanding, or retention.

2. For each idea you have identified, list the type of visual you think would be most appropriate to develop and use.

3. For each visual you have identified, decide on the method you will use to present it.

4. Write a brief paragraph describing why you chose the types and methods that you did. Be sure to consider how your choices will affect your preparation time and the audience's perception of your credibility. You may also fill in the Visual Aid Planning Chart.

You can complete this activity online, download extra copies of the Visual Aid Planning Chart to help you organize your visual aids, view a student sample of this activity, and, if required, email your completed activity to your instructor. Use your Communicate! CD-ROM to access Skill Learning Activity 15.3.

Visual Aid Planning Chart

Idea	Type of aid	Display method

Activity 15.4 Using InfoTrac College Edition (p. 363)
Search for the journal "Vital Speeches." View Vital Speeches and attempt to find a speech on or related to your topic. If there are none, find a speech that sounds interesting to you. Read that speech. Look for ways the speaker attempted to create common ground. Did the speaker use personal pronouns or rhetorical questions? Share common experiences? Personalize information? If you find many examples, how did they help make the speech better? If you found few examples, how would their use have made the speech better?   Discuss what you found below.

Activity 15.5 Using InfoTrac College Edition
Using InfoTrac College Edition, do a subject search using the term "visual aids." Find the article titled "The effect of a nonverbal aid on preschoolers' recall for color, " by J. Ling and M. Blades. (*Journal of Genetic Psychology*, Sept 2000.) Read the article and

summarize the findings below. How do the research findings presented relate to the use of visual aids in speeches?

Activity 15.6 Using Technology

Go to http://einstein.cs.uri.edu/tutorials/csc101/powerpoint/ppt.html and review the basics for using Microsoft PowerPoint software. (If you prefer or if you have different presentation software available at your home or school, use an Internet search engine such as Google to find an online tutorial for your software of choice.) Presentation software can be useful in creating computerized presentations, overheads, slide shows and/or handouts. Using the tutorial, teach yourself the basics of the program and design a possible visual aid for your speech. How can a visual aid of this type influence the audience's attitude toward the speaker?

Activity 15.7 Preparing a Handout

Prepare a one-page handout on "Mistakes to Avoid When Using Visual Aids." The audience will be your speech class. The handout should be clear, visually appealing, focus on main points and reflect an understanding of the material covered in Chapter 15 of your text. Be prepared to discuss and present your handout to your classmates.

Activity 15.8 Evaluating Visual Aids

Using the handout designed in exercise 15.7 or one you have prepared for your first speech, analyze it using the following checklist. Considering your analysis, would you make any changes to your visual aid? If so, what would they be?

Visual Aid Assessment Check List:

	Excellent (A)	Good (B)	Average (C)	Poor (D)
Type of visual aid is suited to the audience				
Aid is visually pleasing overall				

Size of type is appropriate and pleasing to the eye.				
Both upper and lower case type used				
Limit the number of phrases to six				
Focus on information that is emphasized in the speech				
Color and/or clip art, if used, enhances impact				

Activity 15.9 Graphing Numerical Data

Locate an article in a journal, newspaper or magazine that presents data in numerical form. (You may choose to use InfoTrac College Edition or the Internet to locate a suitable article.) After you have examined the numerical data, decide how to represent that data visually. After you have decided, create an appropriate chart. You may decide to create your chart using PowerPoint or other appropriate software. After you create your visual, us a copy of the Visual Aid Assessment Check List to evaluate the quality of your visual. Be prepared to share your visual with your classmates.

Visual Aid Assessment Check List:

	Excellent (A)	Good (B)	Average (C)	Poor (D)
Type of visual aid is suited to the audience				
Aid is visually pleasing overall				
Size of type is appropriate and pleasing to the				

eye.				
Both upper and lower case type used				
Limit the number of phrases to six				
Focus on information that is emphasized in the speech				
Color and/or clip art, if used, enhances impact				

Activity 15.10 What Would You Do? A Question of Ethics (p. 398)
Read the *What Would You Do: A Question of Ethics* scenario on page 398 of your text. Answer the following questions in the space provided here.

1. In a speech, is it ethical to adapt in a way that resonates with your audience but isn't in keeping with what you really believe? Why or why not?

2. Could Kendra have achieved her goal using a different method? How?

Web Resource 15.1: Dr. Joan Gorham (p. 371-372)
For additional information about Dr. Joan Gorham and her work, use your
Communicate! CD-ROM to access Web Resource 15.1: Dr. Joan Gorham.

Web Resource 15.2: Holistic Theory of Speaker Credibility (p. 376)
To read an interesting article that summarizes several theories of credibility, use your
Communicate! CD-ROM to access Web Resource 15.2: Holistic Theory of Speaker
Credibility.

Web Resource 15.3: Visual Aids (p. 392)
For a thorough discussion of the methods and guidelines for using visual aids, use your
Communicate! CD-ROM to access Web Resource 15.3: Visual Aids.

Chapter 15 Self Test (answers and page references in Appendix)

True/False

1. The perception that the speaker and the audience share the same or similar
information, feelings and experiences is called common ground.

2. An important way to let the audience know you are aware of them is by using
personal pronouns.
3. Since chalkboards are usually large, they are best suited for larger, more complex
visual aids that take time to be written down.

4. Since rhetorical questions invite mental participation by the audience in the idea
being discussed, they distract from the speaker and therefore should not be used in
speeches.

5. Timely information will more likely interest the audience.

6. Personableness in the speaker creates distrust in the minds of the audience because
they feel it is a sign of dishonesty or over-excitement.

7. People are more likely to learn when they can see the material as well as hear it.

Multiple Choice

1. The following statement uses what method to build and maintain the audience's
interest? (The audience is a group of college seniors.)

"Have you ever wondered what life will be like after college? Will you be able to get a job? Will you earn enough to afford a house, a nice car, good clothes? Will you be able to save for retirement? Get married? Go to graduate school? Well, today I'd like to help you answer some of those questions by detailing steps you can take now to ensure financial security."

    a. proximity
    b. timeliness
    c. rhetorical sensitivity
    d. demographics

2. In her speech, Karen says: "Let me bring this information a little closer to home. Over 100,000 people a year die of this disease. That's twice the population of this town and five times the population of this college! Some of these people live right here in this community." This is an example of
    a. developing common ground through personalizing information
    b. developing common ground by sharing a common experience
    c. adapting to the audience visually
    d. the use of proximity

3. "The level of trust an audience has in you" is the definition of
    a. attitude
    b. credibility
    c. audience analysis
    d. trustworthiness
    e. none of the above

4. A diagram that shows relationships among parts of a single unit is called
    a. a bar graph
    b. a line graph
    c. an organizational chart
    d. a pie graph

5. Christina wishes to compare the market share of two different soft drink companies to each other. The most appropriate visual aid to do this would be
    a. a bar graph
    b. a pie graph
    c. a line chart
    d. a photograph
    e. a proximity graph

6. Salvatore wishes to show the audience the chain of command of the organization he works for. A useful visual aid for this might be:
   a. graph
   b. pie chart
   c. flow chart
   d. model
   e. none of the above

7. Which of the following is true about handouts?
   a. they can be distracting
   b. they are easy to prepare
   c. each member of the audience can have their own copy of your visual aid
   d. the audience may focus on the handouts when you want them looking at you.
   e. all of the above

8. Which of the following is not true about visual aids?
   a. the more, the better
   b. ideas hard to explain verbally might be easily explained visually
   c. the size of the audience influences the type of visual aid used and the method of displaying it.
   d. all the statements are true

Essay

1. Discuss several ways in which a speaker may build her or his credibility with an audience.

2. What are the different types of visual aids and how can visual aids help improve a speech?

Helpful Links

http://www.public-speaking.org/public-speaking-articles.htm - **Audio Visual and Props**
The Advanced Public Speaking Institute contains a series of articles on the use of visual aids.

http://www.ukans.edu/cwis/units/coms2/vpa/vpa7.htm - **Using Visual Aids**
Tips on using visual aids from the Virtual Presentation Assistant at the University of Kansas.

http://sorrel.humboldt.edu/~jmf2/floss/visual-aids.html - **Using Visual Aids**
Types of visual aids and tips for using them, with some Internet-based examples.

http://www.fastcompany.com/online/07/130crash.html - **When Your Presentation Crashes...**
Tips on giving a "catastrophe free" presentation when using visual aids and technology by Eric Matson.

http://einstein.cs.uri.edu/tutorials/csc101/powerpoint/ppt.html - **PowerPoint Tutorial**
An online tutorial for using Microsoft PowerPoint presentation software by the Department of Computer Science at the University of Rhode Island.

http://www.presentations.com/presentations/index.jsp - **Presentations.com**
Presentations.com is an online magazine devoted to presentations, public speaking and visual aids.

(See your Communicate! CD-ROM for links to other websites referenced in your text.)

CHAPTER 16: Practicing the Presentation of Your Speech

Learning Objectives

After studying this chapter, you should be able to answer the following questions:

- What is extemporaneous speaking?
- How can you develop verbal vividness and emphasis while practicing your speech?
- What are the qualities of a conversational delivery?
- How can you use your voice and body motions to create a conversational quality to your speech delivery?
- How can you schedule and conduct your practice sessions so that you are prepared to deliver your speech?
- What are speaking notes, and how should you prepare and use them?
- How should you practice using your visual aids so that you are effective presenting them?
- What are the symptoms and causes of public speaking apprehension?
- What techniques can you use to reduce your speaking apprehension?
- By what criteria is an effective speech measured?

Interactive Chapter Outline

I. Developing Verbal Vividness and Emphasis

_____

_____

  A. Vividness

_____

_____

    1. Simile

_____

_____

    2. Metaphor

_____

_____

B. Emphasis

_____

_____

    1. Proportion

_____

_____

    2. Repetition

_____

_____

    3. Transitions

_____

_____

II. Creating a Conversational Quality

_____

_____

A. Vocal Characteristics

_____

_____

1. _____

2. _____

B. Bodily Action

_____

_____

1. _____

2. _____

3. _____

4. _____

5. _____

C. Enthusiasm

_____

_____

D. Spontaneity

_____

_____

E. Fluency

_____

_____

F. Eye Contact

_____

_____

III. Rehearsal

_____

_____

   A. Scheduling and Conducting Practice Sessions

_____

_____

   B. Preparing Speaking Notes

_____

_____

   C. Practice Handling Visual Aids during the Speech

_____

_____

      1. _____

      2. _____

      3. _____

      4. _____

      5. _____

      6. _____

      7. _____

D. Guidelines for Effective Rehearsing

_____

_____

   1. First Practice session

      _____

      _____

   2. Analysis

      _____

      _____

   3. Second Practice

      _____

      _____

   4. Additional rehearsals

      _____

      _____

   5. Ensuring spontaneity

      _____

      _____

IV. Public Speaking Apprehension

_____

_____

_____

_____

A. Symptoms and Causes

_____

_____

B. Managing Your Apprehension

_____

_____

    1. _____

    2. _____

    3. _____

C. Techniques for Reducing Apprehension

_____

_____

    1. _____

    2. _____

    3. _____

V. Criteria for Evaluating Speeches

_____

_____

Key Terms

extemporaneously (p. 404)

_____

_____

vividness (p. 405)

_____

_____

simile (p. 405)

_____

_____

metaphor (p. 405)

_____

_____

emphasis (p. 405)

_____

_____

conversational quality (p. 406)

_____

_____

voice (p. 3407)

_____

_____

articulation (p. 407)

_____

_____

pronunciation (p. 407)

_____

_____

accent (p. 408)

_____

_____

facial expressions (p. 408)

_____

_____

gestures (p. 408)

_____

_____

movement (p. 408)

_____

_____

poised (p. 409)

_____

_____

posture (p. 409)

_____

_____

enthusiasm (p. 410)

_____

_____

monotone (p. 410)

_____

_____

spontaneity (p. 411)

_____

_____

fluency (p. 411)

_____

_____

eye contact (p. 411)

_____

_____

rehearsing (p. 412)

_____

_____

speech notes (p. 413)

_____

_____

learning the speech (p. 417)

_____

_____

public speaking apprehension (p. 419)

_____

_____

anticipation reaction (p. 421)

_____

confrontation reaction (p. 421)

adaptation reaction (p. 421)

visualization techniques (p. 423)

systematic desensitization (p. 424)

public speaking skills training (p. 424)

Exercises

Skill Learning Activity 16.1 Observe & Analyze: Similes and Metaphors (p. 406)
Over the next three days, as you read books, newspaper and magazine articles and
listen to people around you talk, make notes of both the trite and original similes and
metaphors that you hear. Choose three that you thought were particularly vivid. Write a
paragraph in which you briefly describe how and why they impressed you.

Skill Learning Activity 16.2 Test Your Competence: Articulation Exercise (p. 408)
The goal of this activity is to have you practice articulating difficult word
combinations. Use your Communicate! CD -ROM to access Web Resource
16.1: Articulation Exercises. There you will find a list of sentences that are

difficult to articulate. Practice saying each of these sentences until you can do so without error. Then write a short paragraph describing your experience.

Skill Learning Activity 16.3 Action Step 5: Rehearsing Your Speech (p. 418)
The goal of this activity is to rehearse your speech, analyze it, and rehearse it again. One complete rehearsal includes (1) a practice, (2) an analysis, and (3) a second practice.

1. Find a place where you can be alone to practice your speech. Follow the six points of the First Practice as listed on p 416.

2. Listen to the tape. Review your outline as you listen and then answer the questions on the Rehearsal Analysis Checklist.

3.Go through the six steps outlined for the first practice. Then answer the questions on the checklist for the second practice. Continue as needed.

Rehearsal Analysis Checklist

First Practice

Are you satisfied with how well:

The introduction got attention and led into the speech? _____

The main points were clearly stated? _____ And well developed? _____

The material adapted to the audience? _____

The section transitions were present? _____ And clear? _____

The conclusion summarized the main points? _____ Left the speech on a high note? _____

Visual aids were used? _____

The ideas were expressed vividly? _____ And emphatically? _____

You maintained a conversational tone throughout? _____ Sounding enthusiastic? _____ Sounding spontaneous? _____ Speaking fluently? _____

List the three most important changes you will make in your next practice session.

One: _____

Two: _____

Three: _____

Rehearsal Analysis Checklist

First Practice

Are you satisfied with how well:

The introduction got attention and led into the speech? _____

The main points were clearly stated? _____ And well developed? _____

The material adapted to the audience? _____

The section transitions were present? _____ And clear? _____

The conclusion summarized the main points? _____ Left the speech on a high note? _____

Visual aids were used? _____

The ideas were expressed vividly? _____ And emphatically? _____

You maintained a conversational tone throughout? _____ Sounding enthusiastic? _____ Sounding spontaneous? _____ Speaking fluently? _____

List the three most important changes you will make in your next practice session.

One: _____

Two: _____

Three: _____

Second Practice

Go through the six steps outlined for the first practice. Then assess:

Did you achieve the goals you set for the second practice? Yes _____ No _____

Reevaluate the speech using the checklist, and continue to practice until you are satisfied with all parts of your presentation.

You can complete this activity online at the Communicate! web site, where you can download addition copies of the checklist and view a student sample.

<u>Skill Learning Activity 16.4 Test Your Competence: Visualizing Your Success (p. 424)</u>
The goal of this activity is to have you visualize your success by "mentally" imagining yourself effectively delivering your speech. To complete this activity, use your Communicate! CD-ROM to access Skill Learning Activity 16.4. Follow the directions to listen to an audiotape that will help you visualize. Write a short paragraph describing this experience below or e-mail it to your instructor.

<u>Skill Learning Activity 16.5 Observe and Analyze: Controlling Nervousness (p. 425)</u>
Interview one or two people who give frequent speeches (a minister, a politician, a lawyer, a businessperson, a teacher). Ask about what is likely to make them more or less nervous about giving the speech. Find out how they cope with their nervousness. Write a short paragraph summarizing what you have learned from the interviews. Then identify the behaviors used by those people that you believe might work for you.

You can complete this activity online at the Communicate! web site and, if required, email it to your instructor.

Skill Learning Activity 16.6 Test Your Competence: Presenting Your First Speech (p. 426)

1. Follow the Speech Plan Action Steps to prepare informative or persuasive speech. The time and other parameters for this assignment will be announced by your instructor.

2. Criteria for evaluation include all the essentials of topic and purpose, content, organization, presentation, but special emphasis will be placed on clarity of goal, clarity and appropriateness of main points, and delivery. As you practice your speech, you can use the diagnostic speech critique sheet as a checklist to ensure that you are meeting the basic criteria in your speech.

3. Prior to presenting your speech, prepare a complete sentence outline and a written plan for adapting your speech to the audience. If you have used Speech Builder Express to complete the action step activities online, you will be able to print out a copy of your completed outline. Your adaptation plan should describe how you plan to verbally and visually adapt your material to the audience and should address how you will (1) Indicate key aspects of audience that you will need to adapt to, (2) Establish common ground, (3) Build and maintain audience interest, (4) Adjust to the audience's knowledge and sophistication, (5) Build speaker credibility, (6) Adapt to audiences' attitudes toward your speech goal, (7) Adapt to audiences from different cultures and language communities (if relevant for you in this speech), and (8) use visual aids to enhance audience understanding and memory. If you completed the action step activities in Chapter 15, these can be used to form the basis of your written adaptation plan.

Speech Critique Checklist

Check all items that were accomplished effectively.

Content

_____ 1. Was the goal of the speech clear?

_____ 2. Did the speaker have high-quality information?

_____ 3. Did the speaker use a variety of kinds of developmental material?

_____ 4. Were visual aids appropriate and well used?

_____ 5. Did the speaker establish common ground and adapt the content to the audience's interests, knowledge, and attitudes?

Organization

_____ 1. Did the introduction gain attention, gain goodwill for the speaker, and lead into the speech?

_____ 2. Were the main points clear, parallel, and in meaningful complete sentences?

_____ 3. Did transitions lead smoothly from one point to another?

_____ 4. Did the conclusion tie the speech together?

Presentation

_____ 1. Was the language clear?

_____ 2. Was the language vivid?

_____ 3. Was the language emphatic?

_____ 4. Did the speaker sound enthusiastic?

_____ 5. Did the speaker show sufficient vocal expressiveness?

_____ 6. Was the presentation spontaneous?

_____ 7. Was the presentation fluent?

_____ 8. Did the speaker look at the audience?

_____ 9. Were the pronunciation and articulation acceptable?

_____ 10. Did the speaker have good posture?

_____ 11. Was speaker movement appropriate?

_____ 12. Did the speaker have sufficient poise?

Based on these criteria, evaluate the speech as (check one):

_____ excellent _____ good _____ satisfactory _____ fair _____ poor

Activity 16.7 Using InfoTrac College Edition

Using InfoTrac College Edition, locate and read the article "Breaking the language barrier," by Stephanie Nickerson. Answer the following questions.

1. Under what speaking circumstances is it important to speak clearly and slowly?

2. Describe one suggestion offered in the article to slow down your rate of speech.

3. Why do you think Nickerson advocates not apologizing to an audience for speech habits and accents? Do you feel you have any such habits?

Activity 16.8 Using InfoTrac College Edition

Access InfoTrac College Edition. Search to find the journal Vital Speeches. Select and read a speech. Then evaluate the speech using the speech critique sheet from Activity 16.6. How effective was the speech? What change would you suggest based on your evaluation? Write a paragraph detailing your evaluation below.

Activity 16.9 What Would You Do? A Question of Ethics (p. 432)
Read the *What Would You Do: A Question of Ethics* scenario on page 432 of your text.
Answer the following questions in the space provided here.

1. Now that Megan knows Donnell doesn't care for Terry, should she let him give the speech? Why?

2. And what about Donnell? Should he give such a speech knowing that he wouldn't support Terry himself? Why?

Activity 16.10 Speech Analysis

Use the Speech Critique Sheet on the following page to analyze the sample speech provided in your textbook on pages 430-432. While you are reading the speech, cover the right side of the page so you are unable to see the authors' analysis. When your analysis is complete, compare your results to that of the authors. Where do you agree with their analysis? Where do you disagree?

(Note: You will be unable to evaluate the speaker on some aspects of presentation as the speech is in written, not verbal form.)

(Note: You may use this form to also evaluate a recorded version of your own speech or one of the speeches provided on the *Communicate!* CD-ROM provided with your text. An extra copy of the form is provided here for that purpose.)

Diagnostic Speech Checklist

(Check all items that were done effectively.)

Content:
_____ 1. Was the goal of the speech clear?
_____ 2. Did the speaker have high-quality information?
_____ 3. Did the speaker use a variety of kinds of developmental material?
_____ 4. Were visual aids appropriate and well used?
_____ 5. Did speaker establish common ground and adapt content to the audience?

Organization:
_____ 6. Did the introduction gain attention, goodwill and lead into the body?
_____ 7. Were the main points clear, parallel and meaningful?
_____ 8. Did transitions lead smoothly from one point to another?
_____ 9. Did the conclusion tie the speech together?

Presentation:
_____ 10. Was the language clear?
_____ 11. Was the language vivid?
_____ 12. Was the language emphatic?
_____ 13. Did the speaker sound enthusiastic?
_____ 14. Was the speaker vocally expressive?
_____ 15. Was the presentation spontaneous?
_____ 16. Was the presentation fluent?
_____ 17. Did the speaker look at the audience?
_____ 18. Were pronunciation and articulation acceptable?
_____ 19. Did the speaker have good posture?
_____ 20. Was speaker movement appropriate?
_____ 21. Did the speaker have sufficient poise?

Comments:

Based on these criteria, evaluate the speech as (check one):

_____ excellent, _____ good, _____ satisfactory, _____ fair, _____ poor.

Web Resource 16.1: Articulation Exercises (p. 408)
For a list of sentences that are difficult to articulate that you can use for practice, use your Communicate! CD-ROM to access Web Resource 16.1: Articulation Exercises.

Web Resource 16.2: Body Motions and Audience Attention (p. 409)
To read a thought-provoking discussion of how various body motions, including posture, affect audience attention during a speech, use your Communicate! CD-ROM to access Web Resource 16.2: Body Motions and Audience Attention.

Web Resource 16.3: Mental Road to Accomplishment (p. 424)
For visualization tips on athletic performance you can also apply to public speaking, use your Communicate! CD-ROM to access Web Resource 16.3: Mental Road to Accomplishment.

Chapter 16 Self Test (answers and page references in Appendix)

True/False

1. Since being nervous is natural, there is no way to cope with it.

2. "Speaking without having the exact wording of what you will say memorized" is the definition of extemporaneously.

3. Movement can enhance the conversational quality of a speech.

4. Since notes detract from eye contact, they should not be used.

5. You should talk about your visual aid while showing it.

6. The surge of anxiety you feel as you begin your speech is called the adaptation reaction.

7. We convey our enthusiasm for a speech topic through vocal variety.

Multiple Choice

1. The statement "The snow covered the city like a blanket" is an example of a(n)
    a. simile
    b. metaphor
    c. transition
    d. parallelism
    e. precision

2. Saying "libary" instead of "library" is an error in
    a. articulation
    b. precision
    c. pronunciation
    d. expressiveness

3. Saying "What ya gonna do" for "What are you going to do?" illustrates
    a. slurring
    b. dropping word endings
    c. articulation errors
    d. all of the above

4. How many three-by-five note cards would normally be sufficient for a six-to-eight minute speech?
- a. one or two
- b. two to four
- c. six to eight
- d. at least nine

5. What are the three major areas of emphasis for evaluating speeches?
- a. content, presentation and articulation
- b. content, organization and nervousness
- c. content, organization, and presentation
- d. articulation, emphasis and vividness

6. James McCroskey is a well-known scholar in the field of
- a. public speaking apprehension
- b. visual aid development
- c. rehearsal of speeches
- d. speech delivery

7. Public speaking apprehension
- a. is normal
- b. is unusually high in about 15% of the U.S. population
- c. varies over the course of the speech
- d. all of the above
- e. none of the above

8. Ted is giving his speech. His pitch, volume and rate of speech remain constant. He is using "uh" and "um" often. Ted
- a. appears disinterested to his audience
- b. is speaking in a monotone
- c. is not using enough vocal interferences
- d. a and b only
- e. a, b, and c.

Essay

1. Discuss why it is important to achieve a conversational quality to your speeches and the five different components of conversational quality.

2. Discuss some guidelines for using visual aids in a speech. Focus on using the aid, not creating it.

3. What can you do to reduce public speaking apprehension?

4. Review some of the criteria for measuring an effective speech.

5. Discuss the importance of rehearsal and how to schedule and perform rehearsals for maximum benefit.

Helpful Links

http://www.ljlseminars.com/bodyspeaks.htm - **Five Ways to Make Your Body Speak**
A discussion of the impact of speaker's body language on the audience by Lenny Laskowski.

http://www.public-speaking.org/public-speaking-articles.htm#practice – **Practice**
Articles on practicing from the Advanced Public Speaking Institute.

http://www.public-speaking.org/public-speaking-articles.htm#stage – **Stage Fright**
Articles on apprehension from the Advanced Public Speaking Institute.

http://www.ukans.edu/cwis/units/coms2/vpa/vpa8.htm - **Presenting Your Speech**
Guidelines and links to help present your speech effectively from the University of Kansas' Virtual Presentation Assistant.

http://www.speechtips.com/delivering.html - **Delivering Your Speech**
Tips on delivery from Speechtips.com.
(To go to the main page: http://www.speechtips.com)

(See your Communicate! CD-ROM for links to other websites referenced in your text.)

CHAPTER 17: Informative Speaking

Learning Objectives

After studying this chapter, you should be able to answer the following questions:

- What are the tests of presenting ideas creatively?
- How can you proceed to leave the impression that what you have said is new and relevant?
- What key techniques can you use to emphasize information?
- What are the major methods of informing?
- What are the key criteria for evaluating an informative speech?

Interactive Chapter Outline

I. Principles of Informing

_____

_____

   A. Intellectual Stimulation

_____

_____

   B. Creativity

_____

_____

      1. _____

      2. _____

      3. _____

      4. _____

     5. _____

C. Relevance

_____

_____

D. Emphasis

_____

_____

     1. _____

     2. _____

     3. _____

     4. _____

     5. _____

II. Methods of Informing

_____

_____

A. Definition

_____

_____

     1. Short definition

_____

     2. Extended Definitions

_____

_____

B. Process Explanation or Demonstration

_____

_____

C. Exposition

_____

_____

III. Criteria for Evaluating Informative Speeches

_____

_____

Key Terms

intellectually stimulating (p. 438)

_____

_____

creativity (p. 440)

_____

_____

reproductive thought (p. 441)

_____

_____

productive thought (p. 441)

_____

_____

relevance (p. 443)

_____

_____

vital information (p. 444)

_____

_____

mnemonics (p. 446)

_____

_____

acronyms (p. 447)

_____

_____

association (p. 447)

_____

_____

synonyms (p. 448)

_____

_____

antonyms (p. 448)

_____

_____

etymology (p. 449)

concrete (p. 449)

demonstrations (p. 450)

complete demonstration (p. 450)

modified demonstration (p. 450)

expository speech (p. 452)

Exercises

<u>Skill Learning Activity 17.1 Test Your Competence: Creating Through Productive Thought (p. 443)</u>
Use the table below to practice productive thinking. Create a list of all of the speech ideas suggested by these data. You can complete this activity on line at the Communicate! Web Site and compare your list to the model created by the authors.

Table of Annual High School Dropout Rates
October 1999

Characteristics	Dropout Rate
Total	4.7
Sex	
Male	4.3
Female	5.1
Race and Hispanic Origin	
White	4.4
White non-Hispanic	3.8
Black	6.0
Asian and Pacific Islander	4.8
Hispanic (of any race)	7.1
Family Income	
Less than $20,000	9.0
$20,000-$39000	3.8
$40,000 and over	2.3
Grade Level	
10th grade	2.7
11th grade	3.7
12th grade	8.5

Source: U.S. Census Bureau, Current Population Survey, October, 1999.

Skill Learning Activity 17.2 Observe and Analyze: Techniques to Emphasize Important Information (p. 448)
Use your Communicate! CD-ROM to access Web Resource 17.2: "Characteristics of Change Agents," a speech by Billy O. Wireman available through InfoTrac College Edition. Analyze the techniques that the speaker used to emphasize important points. How could the speaker have improved his emphasis? Can you identify specific places and techniques where this aspect of the speech could have been improved? Write an essay in which you analyze this aspect of the speech and make specific recommendations for improving it.

At the Communicate! web site you can print out a data sheet to use as you read and do your analysis. Then you can write your essay on line and e-mail it to you instructor.

Emphasis Analysis Data Sheet

Visual aids	Repetition	Transitions	Humor	Memory aids

<u>Skill Learning Activity 17.3 Test Your Competence: An Informative Speech (p. 453)</u>
1. Follow the Speech Plan Action Steps to prepare an informative speech. Your instructor will announce the time limit and other parameters for this assignment.

2. Criteria for evaluation include all the general criteria of topic and purpose, content, organization, presentation, but special emphasis will be placed on how intellectually stimulating the topic is made for the audience, how creatively ideas are presented, how well the relevance of this topic for the audience is conveyed, and how clearly the important information is emphasized. Use the Informative Speech Critique Checklist to critique yourself as you practice your speech.

3. Prior to presenting your speech, prepare a complete sentence outline and source list (bibliography) as well as a written plan for adapting your speech to your audience. If you have used Speech Builder Express to complete the action step activities online, you will be able to print out a copy of your completed outline and source list. Your adaptation plan should describe how you plan to verbally and visually adapt your material to the audience and should address how you will: (1) establish common ground, (2) build and maintain audience interest, (3) adjust to the audience's knowledge and sophistication, (4) build speaker credibility, (5) adapt to audiences' attitudes toward your speech goal, (6) adapt to audiences from different cultures and language communities (if relevant for you in this speech), and (7) use visual aids to enhance audience understanding and memory.

Informative Speech Critique Checklist

Check all items that were accomplished effectively.

Primary criteria

_____ 1.   Was the specific goal designed to increase audience information?

_____ 2.   Did the speaker show creativity in idea development?

_____ 3.   Was the information intellectually stimulating?

_____ 4.   Did the speaker show the relevance of the information?

_____ 5.   Did the speaker emphasize the information?

_____ 6.   Were the methods use to present the information appropriate for the ideas presented?

General criteria

_____ 1.   Was the specific goal clear?

_____ 2.   Was the introduction effective?

_____ 3.   Were the main points clear?

_____ 4.   Was the conclusion effective?

_____ 5.   Was the language clear, vivid, and emphatic?

_____ 6.   Was the speech delivered enthusiastically, with vocal expressiveness, spontaneously, fluently, and with eye contact?

Based on these criteria, evaluate the speech as (check one):

_____ excellent _____ good _____ average _____ fair _____ poor

Skill Learning Activity 17.4: Speech and Analysis: Women in World War II by Lindsey Degenhardt (p. 453)

1. Review the Outline and Adaptation Plan developed by Lindsey Degenhardt in preparing her speech on women in World War II that are printed on pages 453-454.

2. Then read the transcript of Lindsey's speech.

3. Use the Speech Critique Checklist below to help you evaluate this speech.

4. Use your Communicate! CD ROM to watch a video clip of Lindsey presenting her speech in class. Click on the "Speech Interactive" icon in the menu, then click on "Speech Menu." Select "Informative Speech: Women in WWII" to watch the video.

5. Write a paragraph of feedback to Lindsey describing the strengths of her presentation and what you think she might do next time to be more effective.

You may complete this activity online, print a copy of the Informative Speech Critique Sheet, and, if required, email your work to your instructor.

Informative Speech Critique Checklist

Check all items that were accomplished effectively.

Primary criteria

_____ 1. Was the specific goal designed to increase audience information?

_____ 2. Did the speaker show creativity in idea development?

_____ 3. Was the information intellectually stimulating?

_____ 4. Did the speaker show the relevance of the information?

_____ 5. Did the speaker emphasize the information?

_____ 6. Were the methods use to present the information appropriate for the ideas presented?

General criteria

_____ 1. Was the specific goal clear?

_____ 2. Was the introduction effective?

_____ 3. Were the main points clear?

_____ 4. Was the conclusion effective?

_____ 5. Was the language clear, vivid, and emphatic?

_____ 6. Was the speech delivered enthusiastically, with vocal expressiveness, spontaneously, fluently, and with eye contact?

Based on these criteria, evaluate the speech as (check one):

_____ excellent _____ good _____ average _____ fair _____ poor

Activity 17.5 Using InfoTrac College Edition

Using InfoTrac College Edition, conduct a subject search for "learning," then click on "Learning, Psychology of." Look for articles that discuss "how people learn" and "how people think" to gain additional information that is relevant to informative speaking. Read one or more articles to help you better understand how to prepare your informative speech. Summarize your findings below.

Activity 17.6 Using InfoTrac College Edition

The use of mnemonics and acronyms can enhance your informative speaking skills. How? Using InfoTrac College Edition, type in "mnemonic" as your key word. Find and read the article "ART: acronyms reinforce training" by Diane Ullius. Answer the following questions:

1. According to Ullius, what are two advantages to using mnemonics in public speaking?

2. What are three rules for using acronyms in a speech?

3. For your informative speech, identify any material that could be emphasized by use of an acronym. What is the acronym? Describe how you can use it in the speech.

Activity 17.7 Using Technology

Adding humor to a speech is one way to add emphasis to a point and interest to the speech in general. Visit http://www.public-speaking.org/public-speaking-articles.htm#humor or do an Internet search for "humorous anecdotes." See if you can find a way to add humor to at least one point in your speech. Summarize your efforts in the space below. Be sure to record any necessary bibliographic information so that you may cite your source in the speech.

17.8 What Would You Do? A Question of Ethics (p. 459)

Read the *What Would You Do: A Question of Ethics* scenario on page 459 of your text. Answer the following questions in the space provided here.

1. Is Paul's proposed behavior unethical? Why?

2. What should Gina say to challenge Paul's last statement?

Web Resource 17.1: Thinking Like a Genius (p. 441)
To read about eight techniques to stimulate "productive" not "reproductive" thought, use your Communicate! CD-ROM to access Web Resource 17.1: Thinking Like a Genius.

Web Resource 17.2: Change Agents (p. 448)
To read about what an effective change agent is, use your Communicate! CD-ROM to access Web Resource 17.2: Change Agents.

Chapter 17 Self Test (answers and page references in Appendix)

True/False

1. Information that is new to audience members that the audience perceives they have a deep-seated need to know is called expository knowledge.

2. Since repetition of key ideas is boring, it cannot be an effective form of emphasis.

3. "A hammer is a hand-held tool used to drive nails" is an example of definition by use or function.

4. "Antonyms" are words that have the same or nearly the same meanings.

5.   It is possible for an entire main point, or even an entire speech, to be an extended definition.

6. Audiences are more likely to listen to and remember information they perceive as relevant.

7. Practicing the speech a different way each time should not be done since it makes it difficult to memorize the speech.

Multiple Choice

1. Sara is giving her speech on tobacco production. After she gives a statistic on how much tobacco is harvested each year in this country, she repeats the statistic, pauses briefly, smiles, and says "That's *a lot* of smoke!" Sara is trying to
     a. substitute for a visual aid
     b. enhance credibility
     c. add emphasis

      d. show relevance

2. The letters "NAACP" are one example of a(n)
      a. acronym
      b. synonym
      c. antonym
      d. definition
      e. word association

3. Stuart gives his speech on "How to make chocolate chip cookies." His speech is most likely to be
      a. an extended example
      b. a demonstration or process explanation
      c. an extended definition
      d. an exposition

4. "The causes for juvenile delinquency" is most likely a topic for
      a. demonstrative speaking
      b. extemporaneous speaking
      c. definitional speaking
      d. expository speaking

5. Which of the following are effective ways of enhancing your creativity?
      a. gather plenty of useful information to work from
      b. allow plenty of time for the creative process to work
      c. create alternate choices and different perspectives
      d. all of the above

6. In his speech about new financial aid options for college students, Neil tells his audience that "everyone in this room needs money for college, and this scholarship is available to all of you!" Neil is trying to:
      a. make the topic relevant to the audience
      b. enhance his credibility
      c. demonstrate association
      d. be expository

7. Short definitions
      a. can use synonyms or antonyms
      b. should never be used in a speech
      c. only are done via classification and differentiation

    d. never use concrete ideas

8. Rhonda is giving an informative speech on how to construct a powered model airplane. She chooses to complete some of the model at home and do only part of the work in front of the audience. Rhonda is:
    a. hurting the usefulness of the speech by leaving out some information
    b. using a modified demonstration format
    c. using exposition formally
    d. speaklng by definition

Essay

1. List and describe each of the methods of informing discussed in the text. Include an example of each.

2. Describe how you might organize an informative speech on how to do some simple process (such as a recipe). What method if informing would this be?

3. What are the main criteria for evaluating an informative speech?

4. How does a speaker emphasize information? Why is this important? Provide examples of each method you discuss.

5. Describe the role of creativity in speaking and provide examples of how we can improve our creative ability.

Helpful Links

http://www.mindtools.com/memory.html - **Mindtools memory page**
A site for learning more about mnemonics and other skills used to improve memory.

http://www.etymonline.com/ - **Online Etymology Dictionary**
This great site allows you to research word origins. By Douglas Harper.

http://www.webcorp.com/sounds/nixon.htm - **Historical Audio Archives**
 Audio archives of historical figures. Some excellent speech segments. By Webcorp Multimedia.

http://www.americanrhetoric.com/speechbank.htm - **Online Speech Bank**
An index of over 5000 speeches presented by American Rhetoric.

http://www.public-speaking.org/public-speaking-articles.htm#humor – **Humor Techniques**
A list of links for tips, techniques and samples for using humor in speeches from the Advanced Public Speaking Institute.

http://www.historychannel.com/speeches/index.html - **Speeches**
An archive of great speeches presented by *The History Channel*.

(See your Communicate! CD-ROM for links to other websites referenced in your text.)

CHAPTER 18: Persuasive Speaking

Learning Objectives

After studying this chapter, you should be able to answer the following questions:

- What is the difference between affecting attitudes and beliefs and moving to action?
- What is the value of assessing audience attitude toward the goal?
- What are good reasons?
- What kinds of materials give support to reasons?
- What are some common fallacies?
- What are typical persuasive speaking organizational patterns?
- What does a persuasive speaker do to motivate an audience?
- What are major ethical guidelines?

Interactive Chapter Outline

I. Principles of Persuasive Speaking

_____

_____

   A. Write a Specific Goal

_____

_____

   B. Audience Attitude

_____

_____

      1. In favor

_____

_____

      2. No opinion

_____

_____

3. Opposed

_____

_____

C. Give Good Reasons and Sound Evidence

_____

_____

1. Finding reasons

_____

_____

2. Finding evidence to support your reasons

_____

_____

3. Testing reasoning

_____

_____

4. Avoiding fallacies

_____

_____

D. Motivation

_____

_____

   1. Incentives

   _____

   _____

   2. Arousing emotions through language

   _____

   _____

F. Building the Credibility of Your Arguments

_____

_____

   1. Tell the truth

   _____

   _____

   2. Keep your information in perspective

   _____

   _____

   3. Resist personal attacks

   _____

_____

    4. Give the source for all damning information

_____

_____

II. Methods for Organizing Persuasive Arguments

_____

_____

    A. Statement of Logical Reasons Pattern

_____

_____

    B. Problem Solution Pattern

_____

_____

    C. Comparative Advantages Pattern

_____

_____

    D. Motivational Pattern

_____

_____

III. Criteria for Evaluating Persuasive Speeches

_____

_____

Key Terms

persuasive speaking (p. 464)

_____

_____

attitude (p. 465)

_____

_____

opinion (p. 465)

_____

_____

reasons (p. 468)

_____

_____

reasoning by generalization from example (p. 473)

_____

_____

reasoning by causation (p. 473)

_____

_____

reasoning by analogy (p. 473)

_____

_____

reasoning by sign (p. 474)

_____

_____

hasty generalization (p. 474)

_____

_____

false cause (p. 474)

_____

_____

appeal to authority (p. 474)

_____

_____

ad hominem argument (p. 475)

_____

_____

motivation (p. 475)

_____

_____

incentive (p. 475)

_____

_____

costs (p. 476)

_____

_____

emotion (p. 477)

_____

_____

statement of logical reasons (p. 480)

_____

_____

problem solution pattern (p. 481)

_____

_____

comparative advantages pattern (p. 481)

_____

_____

motivational pattern (p. 482)

_____

_____

Exercises

Skill Learning Activity 18.1 Observe and Analyze: A Specific Goal Statement in a Persuasive Speech (p. 469)

The goal of this activity is to find and analyze a specific goal statement.

1. Use your Communicate! CD-ROM to access Web Resource 18.1: Maintaining the Faith and read "Terrorism and Islam: Maintaining the Faith," a speech by Mahathir Bin Mohamad, Prime Minister of Malaysia given at the OIC Conference of Ministers of Endowments and Islamic Affairs, in Kuala Lumpur, May 7, 2002.

This speech is available through Infotrac College Edition. Identify the specific goal statement.

2. Given the composition of the audience, what do you think their initial attitude was toward the speaker's position?

3. Write a paragraph in which you analyze this goal statement. What type of specific speech goal is this? Does this goal seem appropriate for this audience? Explain your reasoning.

You can complete this activity on line at the Communicate! web site and email your analysis to your instructor.

<u>Skill Learning Activity 18.2 Observe and Analyze: Giving Good Reasons and Evidence
(p. 476)</u>

The goal of this activity is to analyze reasons and evidence.

1. Use your Communicate! CD ROM to access is Web Resource 18.1: Maintaining the
Faith and read the speech "Terrorism and Islam: Maintaining the Faith," by Mahathir Bin
Mohamad, available through Infotrac College Edition. Identify each of the main points
or reasons that the speaker offers in support of his thesis.

2. Are his reasons "good"? Are they supported? Relevant? Adapted to the Audience?

3. Analyze his supporting evidence. Assess the quality, currency, and relevancy to his
reasons.

4. Identify two kinds of reasoning links that he uses and then test them using the
appropriate questions. Are the links you tested logical? Explain.

5. Are there any fallacies that you can detect in his argument? Explain.

You can complete this activity at the Communicate! WEB Site and email your analysis
to your instructor.

<u>Skill Learning Activity 18.3 Observe and Analyze: Motivating Audiences (p. 479)</u>
The goal of this activity is to analyze motivational tactics.

1. Use your Communicate! CD-ROM to access Web Resource 18.1: Maintaining the Faith and read the speech "Terrorism and Islam: Maintaining the Faith," by Mahathir Bin Mohamad, available through Infotrac College Edition. Analyze the incentives that Mahathir presents.

2. What emotions do you think that he hopes to arouse? What information does he present to stimulate emotions. Does he seem to phrase the ideas in a way that elicits those emotions? Explain.

You can complete this activity at the Communicate! web site and email your analysis to your instructor.

Skill Learning Activity 18.4 Observe and Analyze: Persuasive Organizational Methods
(p. 482)
The goal of this activity is to analyze organizational patterns.

1. Use your Communicate! CD-ROM to access Web Resource 18.1: Maintaining the
Faith and read the speech "Terrorism and Islam: Maintaining the Faith," by Mahathir Bin
Mohamad, available through Infotrac College Edition. Analyze the organizational
methods Mahathir uses.

2. How well does his pattern fit the attitudes you believe his audience holds toward his
position? Are there other patterns that might have served him better?

You can complete this activity at the Communicate! web site and email your analysis to
your instructor.

Skill Learning Activity 18.5 Sample Speech (p. 483)
1. Review the Outline and Adaptation Plan developed by Eric Wais in preparing his
speech on Capital Punishment.

2. Then read the transcript of Eric's speech.

3. Use the Speech Critique Checklist below to help you evaluate this speech.

4. Use your Communicate! CD-ROM to watch a video clip of Eric presenting his speech
in class. Click on the "Speech Interactive" icon in the menu, then click on "Speech
Menu." Select "Persuasive Speech: Capital Punishment" to watch the video.

5. Write a paragraph of feedback to Eric describing the strengths of his presentation and
what you think he might do next time to be more effective.

You can use your Communicate! CD-ROM to prepare your critique checklist and your
feedback, then compare your answers to those of the authors'.

Persuasive Speech Critique Checklist

Check all items that were accomplished effectively.

Primary Criteria

_____ 1. Was the specific goal designed to affect a belief or move an audience to action?

_____ 2. Did the speaker present clearly stated reasons?

_____ 3. Did the speaker use facts and expert opinions to support these reasons?

_____ 4. Was the organizational pattern appropriate for the type of goal and assumed attitude of the audience?

_____ 5. Did the speaker use emotional language to motivate the audience?

_____ 6. Was the speaker effective in establishing his or her credibility on this topic?

_____ 7. Was the speaker ethical in handling material?

General Criteria

_____ 1. Was the specific goal clear?

_____ 2. Was the introduction effective?

_____ 3. Was the organizational pattern appropriate for the intent and content of the speech?

_____ 5. Was the conclusion effective?

_____ 6. Was the language clear, vivid, emphatic, and appropriate?

_____ 7. Was the delivery convincing?

Evaluate the speech as (check one):

_____ excellent _____ good _____ average _____ fair _____ poor

<u>Skill Learning Activity 18.6 Test Your Competence: A Persuasive Speech (p. 484)</u>
1. Follow the speech plan action steps to prepare a persuasive speech in which you affect audience belief or move your audience to action. Your instructor will announce the time limit and other parameters for this assignment.

2. Criteria for evaluation include all the general criteria of topic and purpose, content, organization, presentation, but special emphasis will be placed on the primary persuasive criteria of how well the speech's specific goal was adapted to the audience's initial attitude toward the topic, the soundness of the reasons, the evidence cited in support of them, the use of motivational language, and the credibility of the arguments.

3. Use the Persuasive Speech Critique Checklist to critique yourself as you practice your speech.

4. Prior to presenting your speech you are to prepare a complete sentence outline and source list (bibliography). If you have used Speech Builder Express to complete the action steps online, you will be able to print out a copy of your completed outline and source list. Also prepare a written plan for adapting your speech to the audience. Your adaptation plan should address the following issues:
    a. How does your goal adapt to whether your prevailing audience attitude is in favor, no opinion, or opposed?
    b. What reasons will you use, and how will the organizational pattern you select fit your topic and audience?
    c. How will you establish your credibility with this audience?
    d. How will you motivate your audience by using incentives or by appealing to their emotions?

Persuasive Speech Critique Checklist

Check all items that were accomplished effectively.

Primary Criteria
_____ 1. Was the specific goal designed to affect a belief or move an audience to action?

_____ 2. Did the speaker present clearly stated reasons?

_____ 3. Did the speaker use facts and expert opinions to support these reasons?

_____ 4. Was the organizational pattern appropriate for the type of goal and assumed attitude of the audience?

_____ 5. Did the speaker use emotional language to motivate the audience?

_____ 6. Was the speaker effective in establishing his or her credibility on this topic?

_____ 7. Was the speaker ethical in handling material?

General Criteria
_____ 1. Was the specific goal clear?

_____ 2. Was the introduction effective?

_____ 3. Was the organizational pattern appropriate for the intent and content of the speech?

_____ 5. Was the conclusion effective?

_____ 6. Was the language clear, vivid, emphatic, and appropriate?

_____ 7. Was the delivery convincing?

Evaluate the speech as (check one):
_____ excellent _____ good _____ average _____ fair _____ poor

Activity 18.7 Using InfoTrac College Edition
Under the subject "attitude change," click on "Periodical references." Look for articles that discuss how audiences process information. Make a special effort to find an article or articles by Richard Petty. Summarize your findings here.

18.8 Using InfoTrac College Edition

Using "persuasion techniques" as your search term, locate the article "Get your way using lawyers' techniques" by Noelle C. Nelson. Summarize the techniques the article presents and how you may use them in your speech, focusing on the following:

1. How does Nelson's argument about the failure of the prosecutors in the O. J. Simpson trial "to clearly and explicitly ask for what they wanted" fit in with Monroe's motivational pattern?

2. Draft a statement where you clearly and explicitly ask for what you want in your first persuasive speech.

3. How is Nelson's advice to use "everyday language" consistent with the motivational pattern of speech organization?

Activity 18.9 Using Technology

Who better to demonstrate persuasive speaking skills but a lawyer? Watch *The Practice, Law & Order, Family Law*, or some other show that depicts a legal trial. Evaluate the way the attorneys try to persuade the jury to accept their point of view. What do they do to build their credibility? How do they incorporate emotional appeal in their remarks? How do they reason with juries? What do they do that makes them particularly effective or ineffective in their speeches? Summarize your findings here.

18.10 What Would You Do? A Question of Ethics (p. 492)
Read the *What Would You Do: A Question of Ethics* scenario on page 492 of your text.
Answer the following questions in the space provided here.

1. Would it be ethical for Alejandro to give his speech in this way? If so, why?

2. If not, what would he need to do to make the speech ethical?

Web Resource 18.1: Maintaining the Faith
To read an interesting persuasive speech, use your Communicate! CD-ROM to access Web Resource 18.1: Maintaining the Faith.

Chapter 18 Self Test (answers and page references in Appendix)

True/False

1. "Reasons" and "evidence" is the same thing.

2. If an audience is highly in favor of your speech goal, then you should emphasize motivation and practical suggestions.

3. The three tests of good evidence are: quality, recentness, and relevance.

4. Reasoning by sign is does not require observable data.

5. The problem solution format works to clarify the nature of a problem and for showing why a proposed solution is best.

6. The motivational pattern is identical to the problem solution pattern except it deletes the attention step.

7. One reason why an audience may have no opinion is that it is uninformed of the goal.

Multiple Choice

1. Juan is giving a persuasive speech on why we should stiffen penalties for child abuse. He wants to present three reasons why we should do this. His speech is likely to be organized using
     a. problem-solution order
     b. logical reasons order
     c. motivated sequence order
     d. comparative advantages order

2. Leticia argues we should not do what George suggests because "George is an idiot!" This is an example of
     a. an ad hominem argument
     b. a logical reasons argument
     c. a motivational appeal
     d. an appeal to authority

e. an appeal to credibility

3. Gaining recognition is an example of
    a. a physiological need
    b. a cognitive need
    c. a safety need
    d. a belongingness and love need
    e. an esteem need

4. Which of the following is NOT a way to build credibility with your audience?
    a. resist personal attacks
    b. give sources for all information
    c. tell the truth
    d. use a hasty generalization
    e. all are acceptable for building credibility

5. Review the following persuasive speech components:

Proposition "I want my audience to vote for the state income tax measure on the November ballot"

Main ideas:
I. Income from the measure will allow government to increase services.
II. Income from the measure will allow a reduction the sales tax.
III. Income from the measure will provide for state employee raises.
This speech is organized in
    a. logical reasons order
    b. problem solution order
    c. comparative advantages order
    d. motivational pattern

6. The three attitudes an audience might have concerning your goal are:
    a. In favor, no opinion, neutral
    b. In favor, no opinion, opposed
    c. In favor, no opinion, reasoned
    d. No opinion, opposed, reasoned

7. The order of your reasons in a speech organized using the logical reasons order:
    a. is irrelevant
    b. does not matter as long as you have evidence
    c. depends solely on the topic
    d. should include the second-best reason first and the best reason last

8. Which of the following is not a type of reasoning?
   a. reasoning by generalization
   b. reasoning by logical fallacy
   c. reasoning by analogy
   d. reasoning by generalization

Essay

1. How can a speaker use voice and language to add emotional impact to a speech? Why is this important?

2. Why is it important to have good reasons to support your speech goal? What is the relationship between reasons and evidence?

3. What are some common fallacies? Provide examples.

4. How does a persuasive speaker motivate an audience to act? Describe key principles and provide examples of each.

5. What are the different attitudes an audience might have toward a speech goal and why is it important to know this information when preparing a speech?

Helpful Links

http://www2.volstate.edu/humanities/comm/outlining/103perlogicalreasons.htm - **Outlining and organization form for Logical Reasons order**.

http://www2.volstate.edu/humanities/comm/outlining/103perproblemsolution.htm - **Outlining and organization form for Problem-Solution order.**

http://www2.volstate.edu/humanities/comm/outlining/103peradvantag.htm - **Outlining and organization form for Comparative Advantage order**

.

http://www2.volstate.edu/humanities/comm/outlining/103permotivate.htm - **Outlining and organization form for a motivational pattern**.
All the above are from Volunteer State Community College

http://www.ukans.edu/cwis/units/coms2/vpa/vpa5.htm - **Supporting Your Points**
How to support your points from the Virtual Presentation Assistant at the University of Kansas.

http://web.utk.edu/~gwynne/maslow.HTM
http://chiron.valdosta.edu/whuitt/col/regsys/maslow.html
Maslow's Hierarchy of Needs
Two sites offering more information on Maslow's hierarchy and related ideas. The first is from Robert Gwyne at the University of Tennessee, the second from William Huitt at Valdosta State University.

http://www.datanation.com/fallacies/ - Logical Fallacies
This great site by Stephen Downes offers detailed information on virtually all logical Fallacies in an easy to use format.

http://www.apa.org/ethics/code2002.html - **APA Ethical Principles**
The code of ethics of the American Psychological Association.
(See your Communicate! CD-ROM for links to other websites referenced in your text.)

Answers to Sample Quiz Questions
PART I

Chapter 1:
T/F
1. T (p. 5)
2. F (p. 7)
3. F (p. 7)
4. F (p. 18)
5. T (p. 12)
6. T (p. 12)
7. T (p. 20)
8. F (p. 17)

M/C
1. B (p. 5)
2. A (p. 4)
3. B (p. 5)
4. D (p. 7)
5. C (p. 17)
6. B (p. 17)
7. E (p. 15)
8. A (p. 7)

Chapter 2:
T/F
1. T (p. 28)
2. T (p. 33)
3. F (p. 28)
4. F (p. 30)
5. T (p. 43)
6. F (p. 39)
7. T (p. 42)

M/C
1. A (p. 30)
2. C (p. 30)
3. D (p. 31)
4. B (p. 33)
5. A (p. 42)
6. B (p. 43)
7. A (p. 35)
8. C (p. 43)

Chapter 3:
T/F
1. T (p. 52)
2. F (p. 54)
3. T (p. 54)
4. F (p. 57)
5. T (p. 60)
6. F (p. 52)
7. T (p. 53)

M/C
1. C (p. 54)
2. C (p. 65)
3. E (p. 61)
4. C (p. 61)
5. A (p. 63)
6. A (p. 52)
7. D (p. 53)
8. A (p. 55)

Chapter 4:
T/F
1. F (p. 72)
2. T (p. 75)
3. F (p. 83)
4. T (p. 87)
5. T (p. 75)
6. T (p. 77)
7. F (p. 83)

M/C
1. D (p. 77)
2. C (p. 74)
3. D (p. 77)
4. C (p. 77)
5. A (p. 75)
6. D (p. 73)
7. D (p. 72)
8. E (p. 74)

PART II

Chapter 5:
T/F
1. F (p. 112)
2. F (p. 113)
3. F (p. 113)
4. T (p. 101)
5. T (p. 102)
6. F (p. 96)
7. T (p. 101)
8. T (p. 108)

M/C
1. D (p. 96)
2. C (p. 101)
3. A (p. 108)
4. D (p. 110)
5. E (p. 100)
6. D (p. 101)
7. A (p. 106)
8. A (p. 112)

Chapter 6:
T/F
1. T (p. 127)
2. F (p. 124)
3. F (p. 130)
4. F (p. 133)
5. F (p. 135)
6. F (p. 137)
7. T (p. 139)

M/C
1. A (p. 124)
2. C (p. 124)
3. B (p. 139)
4. D (p. 128)
5. B (p. 130)
6. D (p. 136)
7. C (p. 126)
8. B (p. 126)

Chapter 7:
T/F
1. F (p. 164)
2. F (p. 164)
3. F (p. 151)
4. T (p. 163)
5. T (p. 150)
6. T (p. 154)
7. F (p. 154)

M/C
1. B (p. 150)
2. C (p. 150)
3. A (p. 163)
4. D (p. 166)
5. C (p. 164)
6. D (p. 155)
7. B (p. 163)
8. C (p. 154)

Chapter 8:
T/F
1. F (p. 189)
2. T (p. 191)
3. F (p. 177)
4. F (p. 178)
5. F (p. 183)
6. T (p. 182)
7. F (p. 183)

M/C
1. B (p. 177)
2. D (p. 177)
3. B (p. 181)
4. D (p. 190)
5. B (p. 198)
6. A (p. 189)
7. D (p. 192)
8. C (p. 196)

Chapter 9:
T/F
1. F (p. 215)

2. T (p. 219)
3. F (p. 220)
4. T (p. 206)
5. T (p. 207)
6. F (p. 206)
7. F (p. 207)

M/C
1. C (p. 214)
2. B (p. 206)
3. A (p. 220)
4. E (p. 215)
5. E (p. 215)
6. D (p. 218)
7. C (p. 223)
8. E (p. 207)

PART III

Chapter 10:
T/F
1. T (p. 232)
2. F (p. 246)
3. F (p. 246)
4. F (p. 236)
5. T (p. 230)
6. T (p. 232)
7. F (p. 234)

M/C
1. A (p. 246)
2. B (p. 242)
3. D (p. 239)
4. B (p. 239)
5. D (p. 241)
6. D (p. 238)
7. C (p. 250)
8. A (p. 250)

Chapter 11:
T/F
1. T (p. 256)
2. F (p. 256)
3. F (p. 259)

4. F (p. 259)
5. T (p. 261)
6. F (p. 262)
7. T (p. 269)

M/C
1. D (p. 258)
2. A (p. 256)
3. C (p. 257)
4. B (p. 264)
5. B (p. 263)
6. D (p. 273)
7. B (p. 257)
8. C (p. 269)

PART IV

Chapter 12:
T/F
1. F (p. 283)
2. F (p. 283)
3. T (p. 287)
4. T (p. 291)
5. T (p. 294)
6. T (p. 294)
7. F (p. 295)

M/C
1. A (p. 284)
2. C (p. 295)
3. D (p. 291)
4. D (p. 287)
5. B (p. 288)
6. A (p. 294)
7. B (p. 295)
8. C (p. 283)

Chapter 13:
T/F
1. F (p. 323)
2. T (p. 306)
3. F (p. 318)
4. F (p. 314)
5. F (p. 315)

6. T (p. 317)
7. T (p. 319)

M/C
1. D (p. 306)
2. C (p. 306)
3. D (p. 308)
4. C (p. 313)
5. A (p. 319)
6. B (p. 320)
7. B (p. 325)
8. D (p. 310)

Chapter 14:
T/F
1. F (p. 349)
2. T (p. 342)
3. F (p. 343)
4. F (p. 351)
5. T (p. 355)
6. T (p. 359)
7. F (p. 359)

M/C
1. A (p. 336)
2. E (p. 340)
3. A (p. 343)
4. C (p. 347)
5. B (p. 351)
6. D (p. 353)
7. D (p. 356)
8. C (p. 359)

Chapter 15:
T/F
1. T (p. 368)
2. T (p. 368)
3. F (p. 390)
4. F (p. 369)
5. T (p. 372)
6. F (p. 377)
7. T (p. 382)

M/C
1. B (p. 372)
2. D (p. 372)
3. B (p. 376)
4. D (p. 387)
5. A (p. 386)
6. C (p. 386)
7. E (p. 390)
8. A (p. 391)

Chapter 16:
T/F
1. F (p. 419)
2. F (p. 404)
3. T (p. 408)
4. F (p. 413)
5. T (p. 415)
6. F (p. 421)
7. T (p. 410)

M/C
1. A (p. 405)
2. A (p. 407)
3. D (p. 407)
4. B (p. 413)
5. C (p. 426)
6. A (p. 420)
7. D (p. 420)
8. D (p. 411)

Chapter 17:
T/F
1. F (p. 438)
2. F (p. 445)
3. T (p. 449)
4. F (p. 448)
5. T (p. 448)
6. T (p. 443)
7. F (p. 442)

M/C
1. C (p. 445)
2. A (p. 447)
3. B (p. 450)
4. D (p. 452)
5. D (p. 441)
6. A (p. 443)
7. A (p. 449)
8. B (p. 450)

Chapter 18:
T/F
1. F (p. 468)
2. T (p. 466)
3. T (p. 472)
4. F (p. 474)
5. T (p. 481)
6. F (p. 482)
7. T (p. 466)

M/C
1. B (p. 480)
2. A (p. 475)
3. E (p. 477)
4. D (p. 479)
5. C (p. 481)
6. B (p. 468)
7. D (p. 480)
8. B (p. 473)